# Sit Tight & Get It Right

# Sit Tight & Get It Right

## How to Beat the Recession Blues in Ireland

Edited by

Caroline Madden and Laura Slattery

**BLACKHALL**
*Publishing*

Blackhall Publishing
Lonsdale House
Avoca Avenue
Blackrock
Co. Dublin
Ireland

e-mail: info@blackhallpublishing.com
www.blackhallpublishing.com

ISBN: 978-1-84218-171-3

A catalogue record for this book is available from the British Library.

Printed in the UK by Athenaeum Press Ltd.

# The Authors

**Kathy Foley** is a columnist with the *Sunday Times*, and was formerly its personal finance editor. She has also written for the *Irish Examiner*, *Irish Tatler*, the *Sunday Tribune*, the *Guardian* and the *Irish Voice* on current affairs, travel, books and pretty much anything interesting under the sun. Her strategy for surviving the slump is to combine travelling and writing in a bid to have an interesting life on a shoestring. She blogs at www.kathyfoley.net.

**Quentin Fottrell** is Irish correspondent for Dow Jones Newswires and contributes to *The Wall Street Journal*. He is the radio reviewer for the *Irish Times* and contributes regularly to that paper's 'Opinion & Analysis' page. He also dishes out relationship advice on his website, www.WorldWeary.com, and every Wednesday on *The Ray D'Arcy Show* on Today FM. He recently published his first book, *Love in a Damp Climate: The Dating Game ... Irish-Style* (Currach Press).

**Conor Pope** is a journalist with the *Irish Times*, where he is responsible for 'Pricewatch', the consumer column that answers consumers' queries, highlights examples of good and bad customer service and road-tests consumer products. He acts as the consumer agony uncle on Today FM's *The Ray D'Arcy Show* and has appeared as one of the panel of experts on RTÉ's consumer lifestyle show, *Highly Recommended*. In December 2008, he presented RTÉ's *Prime Time Investigates – Service with a Snarl*, an examination of how companies ignore complaints from their customers. He is the author of *Stop Wasting Your Money* (Liberties Press).

**Georgina Heffernan** has worked as fashion editor of *U magazine*, *Irish Tatler* and the *Irish Daily Mail*. She has appeared as a fashion expert on TV programmes including *Off the Rails* and *The Afternoon Show*. She has also worked as fashion director on films by Zanzibar Productions, acted as a PR consultant, styled advertising campaigns for the likes of Nike, produced fashion shows for companies including Lee Jeans and styled pop star Macy Gray. Georgina is now working as a freelance fashion stylist, journalist and lecturer.

**Eoin Lyons** writes for the *Irish Times*, the *Sunday Times* Style section, *Image Interiors* and *Living*, among other publications, and also advises on interior decoration projects. He has written two books: *Style Source – Interiors* and *Home Comforts* (Currach Press).

**Michael Kelly** is a freelance contributor to the *Irish Times* and the author of *Trading Paces – From Rat Race to Hen Run* (O'Brien Press). He writes a blog on food, self-sufficiency and growing your own food at www.michaelkelly.ie. He worked for ten years in the IT industry in Dublin but now lives the good life with his good wife in a leaky cottage on a windswept acre in County Waterford.

**Kilian Doyle** is an *Irish Times* journalist. He has been writing the 'Emissions' column in the newspaper's motoring supplement for the past six years, in which he rants and raves about whatever takes his fancy, while actually trying to make a salient point. He sometimes succeeds.

**Edel Coffey** has worked as a journalist since 2000. She has written for various publications, including the *Sunday Tribune*, the *Irish Independent*, the *Irish Daily Mail*, *Magill* and *You & Your Money*. She was the flagship daytime presenter for Dublin's only alternative rock radio station, Phantom 105.2, when it was launched in October 2006, and produced and presented her two-hour daily show *Access All Areas*. She is also a regular contributor to RTÉ television. She moved to the role of features executive in the *Irish Independent* in May 2008.

Nobody told **Gareth Naughton** that a credit crunch was on the way when he decided to up sticks and spend all his savings on a year-long trek around South-East Asia and Australia. Gareth worked for the *Westmeath Independent* in Athlone before moving to the *Evening Echo* in Cork, where he was education and religious affairs correspondent. He currently writes the 'Money Talks' personal finance column for the *Sunday Tribune*. His favourite place in the world is Melbourne, his least favourite is the bank manager's office.

**Tom McGuinness** is managing partner of the McGuinness Killen Partnership, an independent consultancy that specialises in helping organisations and people through transition and change. He is an experienced investigator, facilitator and mediator, and was formerly the chief executive of the Irish Productivity Centre. He has Master's degrees in Organisational Behaviour and Industrial Engineering.

**Andrew McCann** is the author of *Know Your Rights: A Simple Guide to Social and Civic Entitlements in Ireland,* published annually by Blackhall Publishing. He is a regular contributor to both TV and radio across a broad spectrum of issues, including employment and consumer rights, family law, taxation, social welfare entitlements, and other civic and social entitlements. Andrew is the development manager in Fingal Citizens Information Service, which serves north County Dublin.

**Caroline Madden** writes regularly on personal finance issues for the *Irish Times*. Before going into journalism, she worked in the accountancy firm Ernst & Young and qualified as a tax consultant. She is co-author, with Laura Slattery, of *The Money Book: Everything You Ever Wanted to Know about Your Finances (but Were Afraid to Ask)* (Blackhall Publishing).

**Laura Slattery** is a journalist with the *Irish Times* and was the newspaper's personal finance correspondent for a period of five years, during which time she never followed her own advice. She writes for the *Irish Times* business pages and has also written about health, food, fashion and other consumer issues. She currently reports on the trials, and occasionally the tribulations, of the Irish economy. She is co-author, with Caroline Madden, of *The Money Book* and blogs at www.irishtimes.com/blogs/business.

**Ian Mitchell** has spent almost 30 years as a pensions adviser, working both in the corporate and private client environment. In 2003, Ian became managing director of Deloitte Pensions & Investments Limited. He maintains some semblance of a work-life balance through watching sport from various armchairs and enjoying the company of friends over dinner and a glass or two of red wine. He is the author of the book *How to Safely Quit the Day Job: Retiring Early in Economically Tough Times* (Blackhall Publishing).

# Acknowledgements

The editors would like to thank our friends and families for their support and encouragement, in particular Anne-Louise Foley, John Delahunty, Tom Murphy and everyone at the *Irish Times* finance desk. We are also grateful to Elizabeth Brennan and Sarah Franklin of Blackhall Publishing for their help. A special thanks is due to all of the writers who contributed to this book.

# Contents

# Weathering the Storm

Blame it on the builders, blame it on the banks or blame it on the two Brians, but there's no denying that the boom has officially turned to bust.

The Celtic Tiger has been laid to rest and the country's reaction has gone through the classic stages of mourning. First there was denial. Remember when the powers-that-be kept reiterating the mantra about the fundamentals of the economy (whatever they are) being sound? True, the reappearance of the word 'recession' in our vocabulary was unnerving, but although we started shopping in Lidl it was more of a Marie-Antoinette-style novelty than a financial necessity.

But pretty soon the recession proper started to bite, the economists and politicians dropped all talk about soft landings and changed their tune to 'we are where we are', and the nation's reaction moved on to the second stage: anger. And justifiable anger.

If you're like the majority of the population, then chances are you're angry at the lack of leadership shown during the biggest crisis of our generation; angry that, instead of being punished, the banks that fuelled the property bubble with reckless lending are being bailed out, and angry at the lack of regulation of those banks. Maybe you're angry because you didn't share in the spoils of the boom era, yet you're expected to share the pain of solving an economic problem that you didn't cause.

In early 2009, when redundancy announcements became almost a daily occurrence, we tried bargaining: we agreed to take pay cuts if it meant we could keep our jobs; we promised ourselves that we would curb our shopping impulses if it meant we could survive the slump fully solvent. But even the most optimistic among us found it hard not to succumb to the constant barrage of doom and gloom, and we sank into the next stage: depression.

Some people reacted to this by deliberately sticking their head in the sand – they stopped reading downbeat articles, they turned off the radio every time the discussion turned gloomy and banned *Prime Time* from their television sets. But tempting as it is to ignore the bad news and hope that things will simply blow over, acceptance – the final stage of mourning – is the key to beating the recession blues. Acceptance that the Celtic Tiger days are over, but also acceptance that those who will fare best during the recession are those who adapt to it, rather than ignore it.

There are many external economic forces that you can't control, but there are changes you can make to recession-proof your life. This book will hopefully serve as your guide to weathering the storm.

In the introductory chapter, Kathy Foley calls upon recession-phobes to display some Dunkirk spirit in the face of adversity, and dispels the myth that recession living won't be any fun.

A recession book wouldn't be complete without advice on belt-tightening. The main message of the first section is that smarter, more discerning and more imaginative spending can save you money. In Chapter 2, Quentin Fottrell suggests that we fight back against the recession with our wallets, but we must learn to shop smarter and reacquaint ourselves with the value of a euro first. In Chapter 3, consumer champion Conor Pope offers fail-safe tips on savvy supermarket shopping that could save you as much as €2,000 a year. Want to find out how to look effortlessly chic on a shoestring? Every wannabe recessionista should read Chapter 4 by stylist Georgina Heffernan, who proves that a financial slump is no excuse for turning into a fashion frump. When it comes to property, the spirit of the moment is to renovate rather than relocate. In Chapter 5, Eoin Lyons explains how to create a home that will boost your mood without spending a fortune.

The second section of the book looks at ways of adapting your lifestyle to the new economic reality. Find out why producing your own food is one of the most practical things you can do to take the edge off the recession in Chapter 6, in which Michael Kelly makes a compelling argument in favour of self-sufficiency. Kilian Doyle extols the virtues of 'bangernomics' in Chapter 7, the art of buying perfectly good old cars at knockdown prices and keeping them running until it no longer makes financial sense to do so.

Edel Coffey reminds us in Chapter 8 that culture feeds the soul and is more important than ever in times like this. She explains how to access cut-price culture, from cinema to cuisine to comedy. If you're experiencing an irrepressible urge to escape the doom and gloom, even temporarily, then flick to Chapter 9. Gareth Naughton gives the low-down on budget travel, whether you're planning two weeks in the sun or opting out of real life for a year to go backpacking.

The third section of the book looks at managing your money and addresses the more serious financial consequences of the recession. In Chapter 10, Tom McGuinness insists that there is life after redundancy and provides advice on how to deal with the emotional trauma of job loss, as well as direction on how to achieve success in your future career.

If you've lost your job or simply want to claim your full entitlements, then Chapter 11 is a must-read. Andrew McCann of Fingal Citizens Information Service gives advice on how to figure out what State supports are available to you and how to reduce your tax bill.

Want to ditch your old credit-fuelled lifestyle but can't seem to kick the debt habit? Considering joining the 'buy now, pay now' brigade but struggling to pay off your existing loans? Find out how to deal with debt in Chapter 12, written by personal finance journalists Laura Slattery and Caroline Madden. In the final chapter, Deloitte pensions and investment expert Ian Mitchell shares his views on how to invest in financially dangerous times, covering everything from minimising the risk that you might lose all your money to finding opportunities that may arise out of the volatile economic climate.

And that's a key message. When this recession ends (and it will end some day), tales will inevitably emerge of people who prospered during the downturn because they decided to seize opportunities rather than wallow in defeatism. Why not become one of these success stories? After all, as President Barack Obama's Chief of Staff Rahm Emanuel said, you should never let a good crisis go to waste.

# 1

# After the Ball Is Over: Facing into Leaner Times

**Kathy Foley**

*After the ball is over, after the break of morn,*
*After the dancers' leaving, after the stars are gone,*
*Many a heart is aching, if you could read them all —*
*Many the hopes that have vanished after the ball.*
'After the Ball', Charles K. Harris, 1891

You might remember that, for a while there, Ireland was the best at everything. Our little country was the bonny, apple-cheeked kid in the class who got As in every subject and won all the trophies on sports day too. If there was a league table, we topped it. We had the fastest economic growth, the most growth in productivity, the highest rate of employment and the most foreign direct investment per capita. We were the most likely to be entrepreneurs and homeowners. To top it off, some studies even declared that Ireland was the country with the best quality of life. In short, Ireland was only brilliant.

Everyone wanted to be us, not because of our supposedly poetic souls and lyrical way with words – as used to be the case – but because we were a rip-roaring success. We went from being bereft and poverty-stricken (the 'Poorest of the Rich', said the cover of *The Economist* magazine in 1988) to absolutely rolling in it ('Europe's Shining Light', said the cover of *The Economist* in 1997). We were justifiably smug. We gloated. We shopped. We went gallivanting insouciantly around the world, buying up properties in countries we hardly knew existed and generally splashing the cash with the fervid enthusiasm only the nouveau riche can muster.

And then it was over. When Ireland became the first Eurozone country to slide into recession in 2008, we were like fans who didn't want to accept that the player who just scored was offside – it was hard to curb our (by this stage) natural instinct for swaggering jubilance. 'Woohoo! Ireland's first again! We're number one, top of the heap! *Championes! Championes!* What? Recession? Recession like in the 1980s? Oh right. Shit.'

Forgive the obvious analogy that follows, but living in Ireland during the boom was like being at one hell of a party. It was the most glittering, hedonistic, sinfully indulgent gathering imaginable, with swirling lights, thumping music, fire-eaters, burlesque dancers, acrobats on elephants, and torrents of champagne streaming down great towers of stacked coupés. A heaving, heated mob, we revelled until the point of delirium and then kept right on going. We were seeing double. We were seeing quadruple, but we just didn't want it to stop. We fell down a couple of times, but got right back up again. We thought it would never end. We were invincible! Immortal! GODS!

Intimations of mortality began to creep back when, holding our thunderous heads and clutching our nauseous stomachs, we rose gingerly from our beds and squinted out our windows, just in time to see workmen dismantling the marquee and loading the piles of dirty, ripped canvas onto a truck. Where it had stood, there was nothing but muck, flattened grass and piles of rubbish. Then we remembered that the enormous bill for the party would fall due soon and there was no way we could afford to pay it. We sat down heavily and felt very sorry for ourselves. We might have even cried a little.

It has taken a while to get used to the idea that the recession has hit and, worse, that we are likely to be mired in it for some time. No matter how many infuriating know-it-alls contended that any fool could see the bust was inevitable, the lacerating speed of it still came as a surprise in the end. One moment we were considering the possibility of the good times not actually lasting forever, and the next thing we knew the sky had fallen down. Stock markets went into freefall, banks verged on collapse, and suddenly everyone looked slightly stunned and very worried.

After the shock came the heel-of-hand-to-forehead 'Doh!' moment. As an *Irish Independent* headline roared, 'We Blew the Boom.' We could have been sensible, paid off the credit cards, put a little something away for a rainy day (or a torrential-downpour day) and been ready for any eventuality. But we didn't. We blew it, with the result that we are in a right pickle, with creditors getting antsy and repo men lurking around corners. The unpalatable truth is that things are going to have to change around here, mister.

After engaging in a spectacular credit-fuelled frenzy of spending, we can no longer afford to do whatever we want. We have to rethink our expectations, scale back our plans and forget about extravagant holidays and five-course meals in fancy restaurants. Rococo indulgence is out. Straitened asceticism is in. The prospect of penury is not only gloomy, but daunting. How can we cope in a poorer Ireland?

To get some insight into what life in Ireland will be like once the recession is well and truly embedded, we need only look back at the 1980s, when no-one had a bob to their name and the economic gloom seemed interminable. This recession is going to be like that one. Well, it'll be the same but different. Then we taped songs from the radio. Now we download music illegally from the Internet. Then we had Yellow Pack baked beans. Now we have Tesco Value Balsamic Vinegar. You see? Same, but different.

All sorts of 1980s trends are likely to make a comeback. We can expect the return of hand-me-downs, for example. I remember covetously eyeing my cousins' wardrobes each summer, knowing all that stood between me and ownership of those lemon-coloured pedal pushers was a decent growth spurt. Now, however, it's easy to imagine squeals of horror ricocheting around suburbs at the mere notion of hand-me-downs: 'There is, like, no way I am wearing Aifric's old Ugg boots! Oh my God, it's bad enough you're forcing me to do my own fake tan. I totally hate you.' In time, of course, the kids will learn to welcome the arrival of that bulging bag of pre-loved clothing, or at least tolerate it. They won't have much choice.

Likewise, they'll have to get used to going on holidays to their auntie's house, which is what you do during a recession. In the 1980s, your auntie's house was often just five miles down the road, so it wasn't much of a change of scene. But, if you were lucky, they had a Sodastream, which made it as glamorous a holiday destination as anyone could conceive of at the time. That was then and this is now, the difference being that holidays won't be taken at your auntie's house, but at your auntie's second home. At worst, this will be a purpose-built holiday cottage in Ballycotton or Bundoran. (The consensus of the wider family? 'They're stuck with it. Sure you couldn't give that fecking place away.') But it is more likely to be an apartment in Sunny Beach, Bulgaria, or, if you're very lucky, a villa on a golf course near

Marbella. Admittedly, you don't get to pick it out of a travel brochure, but beggars can't be choosers.

There will be, indeed already are, plenty of grimmer parallels with the 1980s. The rate of unemployment is expected to tip over 12 per cent in 2009, although that's still not as bad as the 18 per cent of 20 years ago. Likewise, we must endure painful tax increases and levies, but an 1980s-style tax rate of 60 per cent is unthinkable, at least at the time of writing. Softened by years of positive economic news, we have to be stoic as headlines document an endless litany of misery. Already we are hearing such words as 'repossessions', 'layoffs', 'redundancies', 'strikes' and 'industrial action' nightly on the news.

To endure it, we must rally around. Or just rally. After all, the protest march is a hallmark of recession. This downturn had barely got going at all before people started protesting. Those making their voices heard early included the elderly, students, teachers and farmers. By the darkest depths of the downturn, however, everyone from accountants to zoologists will be protesting. Dublin's O'Connell St will have to be a dedicated full-time protest zone, with no-one allowed further than Jim Larkin's statue unless they are toting a placard and can attest to holding some grievous complaint against the Government. Anyone professing themselves merely mildly irked at the latest round of cutbacks or tax hikes will be turned back at the barricades. With so many people griping, there'll be no room for dilettante protesters.

Mind you, in order to protest against the Government, we're going to have to keep tabs on who's in government. Anyone who was old enough to vote in the 1980s will probably remember doing so with unerring regularity, as governments toppled faster than dominoes. Economic instability invariably leads to political instability, which tends to have the inevitable consequence of less decisive leadership just when we need the opposite. The only consolation is that all those elections will provide plenty of free entertainment during the dog days of recession.

Politicians will have to work extra hard to win votes, though, because the electorate is going to contract. After years of burgeoning inward migration, Ireland is forecast to have net outward migration of fifty thousand in 2009, the highest level in twenty years. The old scourge of emigration is back, but it won't be quite the tragedy it once was.

One news story from November 2008 underscored the difference between the current economic crisis and all those we've suffered in the past. 'Emigrants Abandoning Luxury Cars at Airport', trumpeted the headline above a story explaining that Dublin Airport Authority had to retain a contractor to remove cars left in its car parks by recent emigrants. The abandoned models included 5-Series BMWs. Whatever the chances that even one 1980s emigrant washed their hands of a shiny new Cortina when departing Irish shores, it's unlikely anyone boarded a famine ship having left a thoroughbred donkey and gold-plated cart on the quayside.

Emigration is also cheaper now. A flight to London can cost as little as 1 cent – not including charges for such fanciful extras as baggage and checking in – rather than a week's wages as it did 20 years ago. Furthermore, having a friend or family member leave to work in another country won't be the same wrench it was before. Once they've left, it won't really feel like they're gone at all, as they'll be emailing, instant messaging, Skypeing and Facebooking every day. In fact, you may start to wish they would come back to live in Ireland, as then they might leave you in peace for five bloody minutes.

Some of those who leave will be migrants who came here to make a better life, but get to thinking they may as well be skint and miserable in their home country. Many of those who came will stay, however. Whatever the similarities between this recession and the last one, drab monocultural Ireland is gone. Some of the glitzy boutiques and watering holes favoured by the Celtic Tiger cubs may have to shut up shop, but we'll still have Korean karaoke restaurants, Nigerian hair salons and Lithuanian food shops.

Just as the ethnic makeup of Irish people changed in the past 20 years, so too did the physical landscape. From sprawling housing estates to gleaming office blocks and out-of-town retail parks, it didn't matter what street or road you travelled down, someone was building something on it during the boom. Construction accounted for a fifth of the economy and everyone talked about property all the time – house prices, rents, interest rates, investment properties, yields and margins. We were a people obsessed with building and buying property. Property-related one-upmanship became a national pastime. No sooner had you put a deposit on a buy-to-let apartment in Clonee, than someone would leap to tell you how they had doubled their money in a leveraged commercial property deal involving some warehouses in Belgium.

Given the current parlous state of the property market, one-upmanship's not going to be *de rigueur* anymore. Expect plenty of one-downmanship, however.

Example of one-downmanship:
John:        My house is worth €100,000 less than it was this time last year.
Pat:         That's nothing. I'm in negative equity. My house is worth €100,000 less than I borrowed to buy it.
Tom:         My house has been repossessed. Me, the wife and kids have been camping on Dollymount Strand for the past three weeks.
John and Pat: You win.

Other Irish habits will die harder. Begrudgery, for example, can only thrive during the downturn. Plenty of people will be bitter and resentful they didn't make the most of the good times while they had the chance. The rising tide of the Celtic Tiger may have lifted all boats, but some sailed majestically on the crests of waves, while others bobbed around pleasantly in the troughs. A cadre of Irish society rendered itself recession-proof and will probably spend the next few years delightedly splurging on yachts and helicopters on sale at knockdown prices. Most of us, however, will have to dispense with the 'It' bags and top-of-the-range iPod docking stations.

It'll be tough because we loved to shop. Oh, how we loved to shop before the country's fortunes went pear-shaped. No more saints and scholars, we were shoppers and spenders. In our defence, we may actually have been sick, crippled by a little-known medical condition called oniomania, also known as compulsive buying disorder. Oniomaniacs are preoccupied with shopping and have senseless and irresistible urges to buy things they can't afford or don't need. The act of purchasing makes them euphoric and they can't conceive of life without credit cards. It is thought to affect up to 6 per cent of the American population, which is moderate considering that about 90 per cent of Irish people seemed afflicted with it at the height of the boom.

Yes, we were sick and the recession will be like enforced bed rest, a period of recuperation to get over the ravages of the disease. We'll take our medicine – sticking rigorously to a budget – and if we really can't resist the urge to shop 'til we drop, we'll just have to restrict ourselves to Penneys, Guineys and the Asian super-markets. It will still be fun, even though the prospect mightn't seem too enticing to consumers used to shopping in stores with their own doormen.

That's one of the big worries of recession-phobes – that it just won't be much fun. It's an understandable fear. Life in the downturn will certainly lack spontaneity, at least the way we were used to it. Anyone who makes a cheery suggestion along the lines of, 'I know, why don't we all go to Ibiza for the weekend?' is likely to be greeted with incredulity at best and a punch in the face at worst, rather than whooping cheers of agreement and arguments over who's buying the pills.

But that's not to say recession living won't be any fun at all. The more you throw yourself into it, the more you'll probably enjoy it. Be a trouper instead of a misery guts. Try to thrive on hardship. Relish displaying Dunkirk spirit in the war against spending. Sew your own clothes, grow your own vegetables and insist on foisting homemade gifts on everyone at Christmas. In these difficult times, who wouldn't appreciate a crocheted mobile-phone holder or a flagon of home brew?

Marvellously, such cheap living can also be environmentally friendly. You may have felt worthy back in the day when you used to leave €7 bottles of phosphate-free toilet cleaner prominently on display in the bathroom, but scrubbing the toilet bowl with your own recipe of lemon juice, bicarbonate of soda and fuller's earth will not only be more green, but also cost you far less.

Frugality necessitates ingenuity, but that has its own rewards. Think how much more satisfying it will be to feed the family a menu comprised of experiments with offal and turnips rather than microwave meals. They may revolt initially, but when they're hungry enough they'll be back. Remember, kids brought up on rations during the Second World War were super-healthy. With the junk-free diet and the fact that we'll be walking and cycling rather than paying for petrol or, heaven forbid, taxis, the recession could solve the obesity crisis too. There are always silver linings if you look hard enough.

## Number Crunch

'Staying in is the new going out' is a claim made in the media every now and again, regardless of how the economy is doing, usually because the journalist making the claim has grown a little older, wiser and personally less fond of hanging round the city centre at 3.00 a.m. on Sunday morning. But as Ireland settled into slump mode, it really did appear that people were shunning pubs en masse in favour of either sobriety or 'recession sessions' at home: bar sales fell **10 per cent** in the year to November 2008.

It's a good thing we'll all be feeling so hale, because we sure won't be able to afford to hit the spa. If there is one business sector that is going to suffer during the downturn, it's the wellness industry. It used not to exist at all. Then, suddenly, there were hundreds of spas around the country, each promising a unique, Zen-like pampering experience. What will happen to them, these temples of marble and mosaic tiling, with their treatment rooms, relaxation rooms, mud rasuls and seaweed baths? They could conceivably be converted into medical facilities or affordable housing, but it might be more salutary to let them go to rack and ruin. Like the Roman Forum, their crumbled ruins can stand as monuments to a more vainglorious time.

So, without spa treatments, new cars and all the other accoutrements of the good times, will we be happier or more miserable? Some may find they're genuinely more content after foregoing the endless quest for more and learning to appreciate life's simpler pleasures. Others may return contritely to the Church, hoping for forgiveness and searching for meaning. A major religious revival is unlikely, however. People have managed just fine for the past decade or so without attending Mass every Sunday and anyone with access to the Internet can see spectacles a sight more hair-raising than a moving statue in Ballinspittle.

Most of us won't become hairshirt-wearing hermits or religious fanatics. In fact, we'll probably find life goes on during the recession much as it did before. A famous study published in the *Journal of Personality and Social Psychology* in 1978 focused on lottery winners and paralysed accident victims. It found that most of the participants returned to their earlier levels of happiness a year after becoming rich or ending up in a wheelchair. People, it seems, can get used to just about anything.

It's also worth remembering that the recession won't last forever. If nothing else, our expectations have changed. Like Cinderella, we've seen what can be and, while our hopes may have vanished after the ball, we won't give up entirely. Sure, we'll go back to sweeping ashes for a little while if we must, but we're not going to acquiesce and accept a life of dreary drudgery as our due. It was acceptable in the 1980s, but this time around we know better.

# SMARTER SPENDING

# 2

# The Million Dollar Spit in the Ocean: Fighting Back with Savvy Spending

## Quentin Fottrell

How could I resist? A Vivienne Westwood cream shirt for sale on eBay for just €40. The seller had a photograph of the tag and, oddly, the original bag to prove its provenance. It was a fraction of what it would cost to buy new. It was a steal when it rose to €58 after a chap from Hong Kong bid for it. It was still a bargain at €89. Even when the price of the shirt went to €110 it was less than half of what it would cost in Harvey Nichols or Brown Thomas. It. Would. Be. Mine.

I followed it for days, checking in on the other bidders, in particular that annoying guy from Hong Kong who kept ticking up his bid and trumping mine. I imagined him clickety-clicking every time he saw my latest offer. My blood boiled. The bidding would end on Sunday at 1800 GMT. I set the alarm on my mobile for 1745 GMT. I would have this Vivienne Westwood cream shirt if it killed me. And, as it happened, it very nearly did.

But, first, my reason for buying the shirt. It's the 'million dollar spit in the ocean'. In times of trouble, do a Gordon Brown rather than a Brian Cowen. Whereas Brian Cowen (and Brian Lenihan) increased taxes in the Budget, Gordon Brown did the opposite, slashing the UK VAT rate in a bid to boost consumer spending. The poor cut back in a recession, but those who don't lose faith, and embrace the Law of Attraction and self-actualisation, don't lose their nerve. They pull out their vintage designer clothes, spend wisely, conspicuously and confidently, boost consumer confidence, and keep the rusting wheels of the economy turning. We all know a depression is far worse than a recession. (As the old joke goes: 'I grew up in the Great Depression ... my mother's!')

Consumer confidence is one of the most important financial indexes watched by economists but, crucially, unlike interest and income tax rates, it is something we do have control over. When demand falls, so too does supply, and the fear that the economy might grind to a halt with more job losses becomes a terrible self-fulfilling prophesy. Help keep retailers and restaurateurs in business by supporting them with your patronage.

> ### Number Crunch
>
> Retail sales increased by more than **6 per cent** in 2006, the year in which the first Special Savings Incentive Accounts (SSIAs) matured. Sales volume grew at almost as fast a pace in 2007, as more savers raided their nest eggs and credit-binging consumers joined in the party. But in 2008 nervous shoppers stayed away from the tills, and retail sales fell by **4.5 per cent**, forcing many shops to close their doors for the last time.

Remember the aftermath of the terrorist attacks of 9/11? Both the American and British governments urged people to resist giving into fear and to go about their everyday lives. At that time, Mayor Rudolph Giuliani told New Yorkers to go eat out, go see Broadway shows, buy new cars and take holidays. He told the rest of the world to get on an airplane, book a hotel in New York and help keep the tourist industry alive; in other words, fight back with their wallets.

It's a confidence trick. Think of Scarlett O'Hara when she tore down her bottle-green velvet curtains, fashioned them into a dress, and went to seek help from Captain Butler after the American Civil War. The great mansion Tara, her childhood home, was a broken shell of its former self, raped and pillaged. The trappings of her previous life were gone. But she hadn't lost any of her feisty attitude. She was on a winner until Captain Butler turned over her blistered hands and discovered she'd been toiling on the land.

Drag queens and ageing Hollywood stars understand this. Wigs, gowns, false eyelashes, flattering lighting and – hey, presto! – movie producers don't think you're washed up and the gays come to your cabaret show and believe that, despite their grey, still-unlandscaped apartment complexes, there is hope. But one must be subtle about it: I once told a transvestite she looked like a million dollars. She replied flatly, 'But the dollar is so depressed right now.'

Of course, scouring eBay and vintage clothing shops for the equivalent of those velvet curtains – designer duds that are a fraction of the price – also gives the same dopamine buzz you get from actually splurging on the navy blue blazer with sparkles in one department store, whose sales assistant offered a 10 per cent discount without me having asked for it. I didn't buy that jacket. The off-the-cuff price reduction cheapened it somehow. The thrill of the chase was gone.

Imagine you are a bean counter in Acme Corp. You work with Bob, who is just as good as you if not better, except Bob slouches into the office in polyester trousers, with a hang-dog expression, scuffed shoes and a cardigan frayed in sympathy with his nerves. He worries about getting fired. And it comes to pass. But why not you?

Perhaps the head of Acme thought Bob was lowering the morale, or didn't radiate confidence to its cartoon clients in this crucial time when customers and suppliers are cutting back. Or perhaps he was just a pain to work with, or not as pretty or handsome as you, or maybe the head of Bob's department was mindful of his own vulnerable position in the company every time he saw Bob, and he simply didn't want to be reminded of that.

But that's only partly why the Vivienne Westwood shirt on eBay was important to me. My mobile alarm went off that Sunday at 1745 GMT on a busy, perilous stretch of the N11. And my computer was in the boot. I pulled over onto the hard shoulder and jumped out onto the busy road, dodging cars to retrieve my laptop. I plugged in my Vodafone 3G mouse and waited for 'Connect' to go green. It connected and crashed several times. At last, I opened the eBay site.

At 1758 GMT, the shirt was €178. It was more than I wanted to pay. But still I bid. My screen said, 'Sign into your account.' I had forgotten my username and password. I tried several options. Wrong. Wrong again ... Finally, I logged in. It wasn't about money anymore. This was war. Our man in Hong Kong put in his final bid at 1759 GMT at €180. I was fuming. Heart pounding. Cars flying past perilously close. Hazard car lights flashing. He won. I. Was. Outbid.

Looking back, it would have been a good buy at €58. The feverish bidding for that shirt was a lesson. It was a microcosm of what we've been through during the boomtown years. We stalked MyHome.ie, looking at overpriced, tiny cottages in the Liberties where the owner hadn't even bothered to wash his dirty dishes or, heaven help us, flush the toilet. We all wanted a house of our own to make us happy. A house, even a house of your dreams, doesn't make you happy.

Both eBay and MyHome.ie are about being on top: the adrenaline rush of making bids, asking sellers if they ship to Ireland or quizzing estate agents with harder questions like 'Is this dry rot?' while peeling off a corner of shabby wallpaper. The dry rot set in long ago. We were miserable when we were miserable and we were miserable when we were happy, and we will be happy to be miserable again. The recession has brought with it a tremendous sense of relief.

Here's my rule. Buy smart: designer duds on eBay for a snip. Only if you need a new shirt. Don't buy dumb: a 30-inch high-definition flat-screen TV. Especially if you already have one. Ask yourself questions. What kind of consumer am I? Do I work to shop? Or work to live? When does the enjoyment end and maniacal shopping begin? What are my limits between feeling good and looking good, and being overwhelmed by a thousand ringing cash registers?

I learnt the hard way. I came into the economic whirl-wind with nothing except a part-time job and a rented flat. I came out the other side ... barely. Including interest repayments, I have close to €1 million in mortgage-related debt over the next 30 years, a full-time job, plus several extra-curricular gigs to pay for it all. I am the €1 Million Indebted Man. Without renting out rooms in my home, I will have to work many of those 30 years, day and night.

Tellingly, my walk-in closet is full of unworn clothes. Thousands of euro worth of shirts, jackets, shoes, even a

Russian fox-fur wrap, with its head still attached and two dark soulful beaded eyes, watching me with wry amusement. We have a lot in common. Neither of us could run fast enough to dodge the bullet. Now we are both stuffed, literally and figuratively – prisoners of the past. As an urban fox, as opposed to a real one, it's important to remember: it's only money.

*The Right Hook* on Newstalk 106–108 updates listeners on 'The Happiness Index' at the start of every show, like a weather update. But even those who win the lottery, who become rich beyond their wildest dreams, who can buy the red-bricked period house in Ranelagh with the mature garden or a wardrobe of haute couture, their happiness might peak, but over time it will settle back to near its original level.

Some smart arse recently suggested that the doomster RTÉ reporter George Lee should present the weather. He said it would finally push us over the precipice. I don't agree. I think it would be a tonic for these troubled times. It would be a timely reminder that economic recessions, just like seasons, are cyclical. They will pass over us as benevolent warnings from the gods or rip the roofs off our houses. They're not real tsunamis. We will come out the other end.

The recession also teaches us the value of a euro. We used to have one of the highest rates of private sector credit in Europe. In the men's room of an office block in Dublin a sign read, 'Please use the brush provided if you've soiled the bowl.' It's no small irony that this sign urging us to take responsibility for our own actions was in the Central Bank. Governor John Hurley urged us time and again to cut our debt-happy lifestyles. We didn't.

It wasn't just the peasants who were living like kings. You could see politicians like Brian Cowen eating their fill at the next table in Locks or living it up in the Merrion

Hotel's Cellar Bar. We were all at it. I spotted Mary Harney
and Des O'Malley ensconced in conversation there one
Friday evening, long before the demise of their party. It
was Harney who said consumers have a responsibility to
fight their own corner. She got roasted for that. But she
was right.

And now? The House of Crap, that proverbial palace
where we bought all that stuff we didn't need or didn't like
when we got it home, but never bothered to return within
30 days, has gone out of business. Partly because we
wised up. We must keep our Ernest & Julio Gallo humour,
privately reacquaint ourselves with toasted cheese sandwiches and abandon expensive olive Focaccia with organic
Camembert and rocket. This was how the Irish survived
the Famine.

I don't believe we were ever that comfortable with the
New Money. We thought it would fill that void, heal the
wounds that we have carried on behalf of our forebears
for generations: the years of living under colonialism, the
long divisive struggle for independence, living with
terrorism, the Christmas bomb scares when we fled
department stores en masse, and the bitter tears of
emigration. It all took its toll on our psyche. Shopping
never cured that.

We can regain our collective sense of self. The Irish are
great storytellers. When we were actually poor, as opposed
to without-money, before we identified a lifestyle on Visa
or Mastercard or eBay or MyHome.ie – that lifestyle to
which we would like to become accustomed, but never
really did – we entertained each other with stories. After
the boom, we did the same, but this time the story was
the Grimm fairytale of the woodcutter who blew his three
precious wishes: low interest rates, cheap credit and high
salary.

We will brave this recession by telling tall tales of the good times, reliving them and laughing at our own folly. We could start with those queues outside Northern Rock when the first cracks in the financial system began. They were comically reminiscent of the soup kitchens of the Great Depression. Except the average deposit was €90,000 and the depositors hid from the photographers, believing them to be the Tax Man in disguise.

The recession has also taught us about responsibility and the latch key to fulfillment. If we cannot find what we are looking for in our own backyard, as that girl in the blue gingham dress and pigtails from Kansas once said, then we haven't really lost it in the first place. For instance, that walk-in closet – a room without a view – I know now is a treasure chest of my own discontentment. A reminder that too much of anything won't make us happy.

Advertisers sell happiness. It is a commodity that remains forever out of reach. We are particularly vulnerable as a nation with low self-esteem. Here are some of the symptoms of low self-esteem: status anxiety, searching for the secret elixir of youth, the desire to be beautiful, going to the 'right' school, having someone to call your own, wanting to be loved or liked. Pursuing such ambitions didn't make us happy during the boom. The bubble bursting could yet be the best thing that ever happened to us.

I own a Dior key ring. It is shaped like a flower with petals. It is beautiful. It was given to me by a friend for my birthday, so it has a special significance. But it is also a shiny symbol of the truth that, when our resources dwindle, luxury goods companies will merely sell us a smaller piece of the dream. Maybe not a pair of Jimmy Choos or a Donna Karen golden fleece (in velvet, I have that too), but a Dolce & Gabbana silk tie or multi-coloured Paul Smith wallet.

# The Million Dollar Spit in the Ocean

This trickle-down economics leads me all the way back to Penneys on O'Connell Street on a mid-week afternoon. Groups of young mothers with prams and old ladies in heavy wool coats rifle through the clothes, holding pink T-shirts up to the light, then discarding them back into the bargain bin with a haughty, dismissive air. Even in this harsh light, bad muzak and constant price announcements, I liked their chutzpah.

I recently interviewed George Weston, the head of Associated British Foods, which owns Penneys, and he spoke with respect of those young mothers who shop diligently at what he calls the 'value end' of the consumer food chain. He plans to open twenty new Primark stores in Spain over the next two years. Primark is morphing into trendy Zara. We must do the same as Penneys and re-brand ourselves into mix-and-match, cut-priced, pure-new-wool babes.

However, 'the million dollar spit in the ocean' survival-of-the-phattest theory doesn't on the face of it include places like Penneys. Or does it? What fool would spend €65 on a pair of Calvin Klein Y-fronts that come in a box with a picture of a well-endowed male model on it? The photo shoot may have been expensive, but the Y-fronts cost a fraction of the price to manufacture. We are the ones who are paying for the fantasy.

No one can see your H&M multicoloured underwear. They are a snug fit, but it shows you are smart (and even kinky if you buy the lycra ones) if you shop in H&M for your smalls. I have friends who mix their discounted designer duds with 100 per cent wool or wool-mix numbers from Penneys. George Weston was happy to hear that. The Scarlett O'Hara curtains or eBay-designer-shirt trick shows you can weather a downturn … with bravado and style.

The aforementioned Dior key ring holds the latch key to the front door of my house, with its hearth and backyard, and not to mention the Dyson (and negative equity) stored under the stairs. It may be a small piece of the consumer jigsaw puzzle, which even the best self-assembly storage units from Ikea could fail to organise, but it tells me that we have a lot to be grateful for. We may not be rich. Whatever that means. But neither are many of us poor.

Here's the most audacious example of what I mean. I first noticed it a few months ago when I was buying some Alka-Seltzer in my local chemist. It was a pyramid of pink-and-black boxes called Celebrity Slim, a seven-day meal replacement regime offering shakes and soup for the soul or, in their language, a low-carb weight-loss programme. Whatever happened to eating less and healthier, and exercising more? That's what I call one big wake-up call.

Our Woody-Guthrie-inspired, Lidl-salad-bowl blues have allowed us to rebrand our celebrity-inspired spending habits for essentials, from Y-fronts from H&M to T-shirts from Penneys, not to mention Lidl's global positioning systems (GPS) for our cars, which should bring home the fact that we had lost our way. Middle-class consumers want to be seen to be contented and rich, but now they get to be cheap-chic and clever clogs too. If you don't fork out for Celebrity Slim, that is.

This is the best spit in the ocean yet – Guineys on Talbot Street from time-to-time sells discontinued lines of Waterford Crystal: candlesticks, liqueur glasses, cocktail glasses and bowls. I bought two unused champagne glasses for €25, still in their box. They retailed two years earlier for over four times that. News like this travels fast. Needless to say, up the street, the staff at the Waterford Crystal department in Clerys aren't exactly doing handstands.

We live in the Land of the Cut-Price Hat Boxes. This could be the biggest lesson of all. I came across a shop in Wexford with them. What do you buy when you have bought everything? Hats. And? Hat boxes. After that? More hat boxes to store other things. And? Bargain basement hat boxes. Cardboard boxes are a barometer for the economy. But, in keeping with our theory, who's to know if there's not a Philip Treacy wimple inside? We must learn to waste less.

In the basement car park of the Dundrum Town Centre, one of the largest shopping malls in the country, there are dozens of parking ticket machines. If you put your ticket into the machine after an afternoon browsing John Lewis or BT2 or Penneys (yes, they're there too) three little words flash up on screen: 'Change Is Possible.' It's a bad translation by the manufacturers. But it could also be a timely subliminal message from the other side.

Thousands of people pass through that car park. Some may not notice that message. We all want to look good and feel good. We can, without sinking into paroxysms of grief and recrimination, learn the accidental lesson from that ticket machine: buy quality, stick with our debit cards and put our credit cards back in our pockets.

I eventually settled for a cheaper, blue Vivienne Westwood shirt from eBay, by the way. I still love it. Even though I quietly suspect it's a fake.

# 3

# Never Shop When You're Hungry: Buying on a Budget

## Conor Pope

It's amazing the difference a couple of years can make. Back in the heady days of 2007, Ireland's economists were still talking up the Celtic Tiger's chances of outliving us all and the estate agents were still talking down the chances of the property bubble bursting. For many Irish shoppers, the German discount shops were still strange places selling strange stock to strange people, and the only chicken many of us would have even considered buying was free range, corn fed and allowed to spend its days basking in the sunshine.

Then everything went bananas. The global banking system collapsed – or as good as collapsed – and everyone simultaneously stopped buying or selling houses. Huge numbers of people suddenly wised up to some of the worst rip-offs in Irish retailing and took their business to the German discounters, saving themselves a packet, while others stopped caring if the only light their chicken ever came close to was the little light in the cooker as it roasted. As long as it cost less it was good enough.

### Number Crunch

Sales at the Irish stores of German discount chain Aldi grew by **21 per cent** in 2008 – a clear sign that Ireland had become caught up in the phenomenon known across Europe as 'Aldification'. This takes place when an economic slump encourages consumers to migrate from their usual weekly grocery shopping haunts to no-frills discounters such as Aldi and its rival Lidl – shops that they once sneered at for being downmarket.

And, as last year came to a close, entire towns south of the border would empty on weekends as the citizenry ignored the calls for patriotic local shopping in favour of bargain basement prices (and mile-long tailbacks and queues for shopping trolleys) on offer in Newry.

While some supermarkets operating in the Republic said they were close to closing because of the migration of their customer base, the biggest change in Irish retailing and the biggest challenge to existing retailers in the last couple of years has undoubtedly been the relentless rise of Aldi and Lidl – and the dramatic improvement in the quality of merchandise offered by both. Together, the two stores now have around 10 per cent of the Irish retail market, a number that is set to grow as both companies expand into untapped areas this year and next.

While the recession has played a major role in this shift, the National Consumer Agency (NCA) is also entitled to claim some of the credit. Repeated surveys from the consumer body charged with protecting our interests have been published, which show that Aldi and Lidl are between 20 per cent and 50 per cent cheaper than the more established retailers.

Critically, the NCA also showed that there was virtually no price difference between the State's biggest supermarkets – for one basket of more than 60 items costing over €60, just 35 cent separated Tesco and Dunnes Stores. While the more established supermarkets offer a bigger range of products and more recognisable products, it is a bit dispiriting for many consumers to learn that it appears they are more keen on price matching than price cutting.

It's different across the border, where Asda, now owned by the US giant Walmart, seems to genuinely drive down prices. Supermarket prices in Newry are, at the very least, 15 per cent cheaper than in the same supermarkets a few kilometres away in Dundalk. For some items the price gap is closer to 50 per cent, which is why, in the latter part of 2008, the number of cars heading across the border increased dramatically. However, only the really savvy shoppers made significant savings. The key is to price the products you want to buy before you go on www.sainsburys.co.uk or www.tesco.co.uk, work out what is significantly cheaper and compile a list made up of only these products.

The message that came loud and clear from the NCA surveys was the importance of shopping around and divvying up your spend between the discounters, the big supermarkets – they do still offer some good value when it comes to branded goods and their specials are also worth keeping an eye on – and your local greengrocer and butcher, who can be surprisingly good value.

'Split your shopping basket' has been the mantra for months now and it has been heeded by many, with further studies from the NCA showing that, because of the increasingly wide price gaps, people have changed habits of a lifetime in search of better value. And it's little wonder as, if you are a little more canny about how you shop, you can save yourself over €2,000 a year.

## Chasing Discounts

While the quality of some of the bargain basement products in many of our supermarkets is patchy (revolting might be another, better, word), some items are certainly worth considering – as long as you pay attention to the small print and shop wisely.

At the tail end of last year, Tesco Value baked beans and Campo Largo baked beans from Lidl were both priced at 25 cent, but the Tesco product contained 40 per cent haricot beans and 14 per cent tomato puree compared with Lidl's 49 per cent haricot beans and 27 per cent tomatoes, indicating that the latter offered better value. Tesco Value sausage rolls, meanwhile, were made with 12 per cent pork while their Lidl equivalent had 27 per cent pork; again the prices were the same. Lidl processed cheese slices had 51 per cent cheese while the Tesco Value cheese singles were made with just 11 per cent cheese. Eleven per cent cheese! In a cheese slice! With numbers like that you might be as well steering clear of such products entirely, whatever the price.

If, for instance, you have a cat that likes Whiskas, then you can expect to spend around €450 this year on its food – and well over five grand over the course of its life. Quietly swap it for Aldi's Vitacat Supreme Chunks, and you'll spend only a third of the price. Your cat won't notice – well, probably not. And even if they do, stick with it and they're bound to get a taste for it eventually.

And it's not just the cat that should be expected to economise. If you routinely buy sparkling water and swap the four-pack of 1.5-litre bottles of Ballygowan for a four-pack from Aldi, then over the course of a year you could save yourself around €150 without impacting on the quality of your life one iota.

When it comes to cleaning products, the differences in quality are much harder to discern. In fact, if you don't have to eat it, the difference in price between the premium and the value ranges is crystal clear and always attractive.

In 2008, there were times when a two-litre bottle of Domestos in Tesco cost around €3, while a similarly sized bottle of non-brand-name bleach in Aldi cost slightly over €1. While the makers of Domestos might argue that their product is intrinsically better than the Aldi equivalent, it is hard to imagine it could possibly be nearly three times better. Bleach is, after all, bleach.

It's the same for bin bags, sponges, rubber gloves and a whole lot of other items. A basket of just 10 kitchen cleaning items sourced in Aldi costs over €20 less than similar products made by brands that have big marketing budgets behind them – marketing budgets you're paying for. If consumers were to do a little research and buy just 20 such items in either Aldi or Lidl each week, instead of buying branded products, they could knock around 30 per cent off their weekly shopping bill. Spread out over the course of a year, the potential savings run into hundreds of euro.

While a lot of people are new converts to frugality, it should never be the be-all and end-all, even for the canniest of shoppers. Few people could argue that all breakfast cereals or tea bags – to pick just two items – are equal and life's way too short to spend it eating joyless breakfasts. It is important to remember that there are occasions when quality does count. Take washing-up liquid. There is no-one who could seriously argue that the Lidl or Aldi brand is as good as Fairy Liquid. The august UK consumer body Which? has consistently ranked Fairy as the best product on the market, despite its higher cost. A single one-litre bottle cleans more dirty plates – eleven thousand – than any of its rivals.

The bottom line is to shop smart and selectively and forget the loyalty (but not the loyalty cards – sign up to the lot of them, they'll save you around €100 a year). Being loyal to Tesco, Dunnes, Superquinn or even Marks & Spencer – bless them and their lovely food and less lovely prices – is foolhardy and could end up costing you a packet.

## Costly Convenience

In the last ten years there has been a push on the part of the retailers to drive us to so-called 'value-added' products. Sprouts come pre-peeled and our onions can be found pre-chopped. All the convenience comes at cost and, in these leaner times, it is a cost that is almost always best avoided.

Chicken pieces with some of the skin and bones still attached are about half the price of pre-skinned chicken pieces. Removing that skin and bone takes seconds, and you can save yourself a couple of euro every week handily enough.

Bagged salad is the enemy of the money-conscious. Of course it's convenient but it costs ten times more than making the salad up from scratch and it doesn't taste half as nice – mostly because it has been drowned in chemicals that strip the leaves of dirt and nutrients (admittedly, there are some bagged salads on the market that have been washed in spring water – but do you really want to be the kind of person who eats rocket washed in spring water? No, no you don't).

If you do buy salad leaves, bagged or otherwise, remember to eat them. According to a survey carried out by a British insurance company last year, 61 per cent of people polled confessed to binning a soggy lettuce every week because they bought it under the false assumption that they'd eat more greens than they actually did.

And what about pre-grated cheese? A kilogramme of grated cheddar costs around €15, while a block of the same cheese from the same company costs around €5 less. Presuming that you are already in possession of a cheese grater and working hands, you've saved yourself €2.50 on a single block of the stuff. And, really, who's too busy to grate cheese?

The greatest, most wasteful example of value-added products are on the ready-meal shelves. Ready meals can be five times as expensive as the constituent parts of that meal sitting on the shelves just a few metres away in the same supermarket. And it really doesn't take that much effort to fry a steak and bake a potato, even if the Cook, GastroPub, Finest or Select range has been tarted up to look super-tasty.

**Savvy Supermarket Shopping**

Other shopping tips that will save you money are fairly obvious, but worth stating nonetheless.

It's an old truism that you should never go shopping when you're hungry – you'll end up buying a whole lot more than you intended if you do.

It's time to learn the prices of the basics. How much is a litre of milk or a pound of butter? If you can't answer immediately, how are you supposed to know you're being ripped off when your local corner shop charges you €2.50 for the milk and €4 for the butter?

Supermarkets have worked out the best ways to get us to part with our cash and, while we may think we're immune to the soothing background music, the judiciously placed 'offers' and the smell of baking that wafts through the aisles, the bill at the checkout would beg to differ. That's why it's important to make lists and stick rigidly to them. Not only will it be cheaper, but it'll make the trip to the supermarket a lot shorter too.

And don't just make lists of your shopping. Each week sit down and plan your weekly menu. It takes five minutes, unless you're a Michelin-starred chef, in which case your imagination might ensure it takes a little longer. Anyway, plan the menu and only buy what you need for the menu. It will cut down on impulse buys and dramatically reduce the amount of food you throw away each year.

Impulse shopping is the undoing of the budget-conscious – not to mention a sure way of accumulating vast quantities of junk in your house. Don't allow yourself to fall victim to this pernicious habit. Never buy clothes on the spur of the moment; instead, give yourself a 24-hour cooling-off period and if, after that time, you still find yourself thinking about those boots or that mulcher, then go ahead and make the purchase by all means, but not before you check out the Web to see if you can get it cheaper elsewhere.

**Click Here for Bargains**

High prices, limited choice, and the elbows and umbrellas of thousands of competing shoppers are the principal reasons why Irish consumers continue to turn away from traditional retailers and go online in search of bargains. Repeated surveys show that, across the EU, Irish people are second only to the Germans when it comes to buying online. And according to one survey from Deloitte, more than a third of shoppers used the Web as a source of cheaper gifts during Christmas 2008.

CDs, DVDs, books and cameras routinely cost at least 20 per cent less online – even when delivery charges are factored in.

High-street shops blame higher overheads here and differing tax regimes across the EU for the significant price disparities. And while they may have a point, should that really be of any concern to consumers who have grown weary of being bled dry?

From the functionality and reliability of Amazon (www. amazon.co.uk) to the quirkiness and enormous potential to snag an amazing bargain of eBay (www.ebay.ie), the Internet has grown into a genuinely global marketplace – and one which people would be foolish not to exploit. Moreover, local retailers have taken to the Web and are passing on great savings to their customers as well.

When it comes to buying books and CDs, it is hard to top Amazon for choice and bargains, although CD Wow (www.cdwow.ie) is okay when it comes to CDs. Not long ago, researchers from British consumer group Which? filled a shopping basket with eight electrical items, including TVs and MP3 players, and found that, by shopping online, they could save more than £1,000. Even when delivery to Ireland is taken into account, things cost at least 20 per cent less when they are bought online.

Unfortunately, Amazon stubbornly refuses to deliver electronic goods to the Republic. The company says it is unable to deliver these items because of difficulties the site has apparently encountered with the Waste Electronic and Electrical (WEE) recycling system in place here, but we have our doubts, particularly as the body responsible for WEE in Ireland has specifically stated that online traders based in other jurisdictions are exempt from the scheme. Weirdly, computer software, PC and video games, toys, games and video items, which are neither electrical nor electronic, are also not available to shoppers from the Republic.

Some companies do ship electronic goods to the Republic of Ireland at very competitive prices, including Pixmania (www.pixmania.com), Dabs (www.dabs.com) and Komplett (www.komplett.ie).

In addition to the savings that can be made and the convenience of shopping from your home (or office – although never during working hours, naturally), buying online means that the websites can wrap and send the items directly to far-flung relatives and friends, saving you the bother of a trip to the post office or even looking for Sellotape.

And then there is eBay, the friend (and the arch-enemy, incidentally) of budget-watchers. With an Irish person reportedly buying something on the site every 20 seconds, it has become the first port of call for many canny consumers in search of everything from household furniture to computer equipment, baby buggies and vintage clothes.

Having bought an oak dining-room table in the sales for €1,000 a couple of years back, I was dismayed to learn that matching chairs would cost €300. That's €300 each. With a set of six costing almost double the price of the table, I decided to go online, where I found six solid-oak Victorian chairs in perfect condition. I bought the lot in an auction for €350. After adding the €150 delivery charge from the UK, the total was still €1,300 less than it would have cost to buy new chairs in Dublin. And they were delivered to my door nearly two months earlier than the department store could have managed.

It's not just in auctions that eBay bargains can be found. While the site is great for second-hand items, there is also good value to be found on the millions of brand-new products populating its virtual shelves and selling for fixed 'buy it now' prices. MP3 players and their accessories can be bought for half-nothing; iPod speakers, which

36

currently sell for more than €100 in Ireland, can be bought and shipped from the Far East for a tenth of that price.

A Canon Digital SLR camera from the US currently has a 'buy it now' price of just over €600, similar to its cost in Ireland. However, the eBay deal also includes a tripod, an additional 70–300mm lens, extra memory and a camera bag, with a total value of more than €500. This is very good value, even considering the duty that Customs and Excise might slap on if your parcel is stopped and examined.

Although there are substantial savings to be made, it would be naive to suggest that shopping online is risk-free. Buying certain items – notably art, clothes and jewellery – without having any physical contact either with the item or the seller is obviously problematic. Taxes, when they are rigorously applied, and the charges imposed by delivery companies – which sometimes administer the taxes – can eat into the potential savings. Timely delivery is also a concern.

It is worth remembering, however, that the prices initially quoted may be misleading, as you still have to pay for shipping and, if you buy from outside the EU, you are liable for all taxes and duties in this country.

**Quell Your Consumer Cravings**

When it comes to shopping, however, the best and most enduring tip to help you survive in these recessionary times is quite simple: don't. Don't actually buy anything. Don't window shop or lust after 'It' bags and 'in' clothes and zeitgeisty gizmos and new cars and bigger houses that you really don't need. If you can toughen yourself up and teach yourself to crave less, then ultimately you'll be happier and wealthier and a whole lot more chilled out than the conspicuous consumer you might otherwise have been. And with all the savings you'll make from developing this Zen-like disregard for stuff, you'll be able to afford at least two holidays in the Caribbean every year.

# 4

# Style on a Shoestring

## Georgina Heffernan

With all this gloomy talk of recession, the fashion world has had to embrace a different attitude to fit the new mood. After years of worshipping at the altar of consumerism, it's time to bid farewell to the gluttonous consumer epitomised by the label-flaunting, fake-tanned, 'It'-bag-carrying 'fashionista' (I never liked her anyway). Now it's time to say hello to her environmentally friendly, down-to-earth, yet surprisingly stylish sister – the 'recessionista'.

Yes, a new breed of cash-conscious woman is stalking the Irish high street.

### The Recessionista

The so-called recessionista may look as though she has spent a fortune on her wardrobe, but her outfit was probably picked up from a sale rail or the local branch of Oxfam. First used in New York fashion circles, the term describes a woman who seems unaffected by the credit crunch. She has a fabulous new look for every occasion and still manages to look effortlessly elegant, even on a modest income. Read on – because I'm about to share her style secrets with you.

Fashion is a topsy-turvy world. Only a few years ago, wearing clothes bought from a charity shop was tantamount to fashion death. Your outfit had to be new and brash, the label identifiable from a hundred paces. But if you're still one of those saddos who thinks that wearing designer labels means you have 'style', then I have some very bad news for you. These days, it's far more hip to be seen rifling through the local charity shop than browsing the rails at some overpriced boutique. Suddenly it's chic to be thrifty, cool to count your pennies and stylish to save.

Cheap and chic is the new mantra for cash-strapped shoppers, and the great news is that it's really never been easier to look good on a budget, once you know how. A designer look need not cost hundreds. In fact, from a charity shop it can cost less than €30. You can also pick up amazing fashion finds at car boot sales, jumble sales, local markets, websites like eBay, or clothes-swap parties. You can choose to customise your clothes or even make your own.

### Number Crunch

Fashion is not so fast any more: sales of clothes sank almost **7 per cent** in the year to November 2008, spurring retailers to introduce bigger discounts to offload their stock. As consumers turned away from the changing rooms, department stores such as Marks & Spencer held their first ever 'guerrilla sales', offering one-day discounts of up to **20 per cent**. On average, the price of clothing and footwear in Ireland fell **6.5 per cent** in 2008, making trawling through the clothes rails a less costly habit.

In the wake of a wobbly economy, bank collapses and falling house prices, here is a trend that appeals to our newfound 'smart consumerist' sense of getting more bang per buck. Yes, I'm talking about being thrifty. So please forgive me if I'm beginning to sound a little like your Mum. But sometimes she does make sense.

## Thriftiness

The word 'thriftiness' has got a penny-pinching, Victorian, tight-lipped quality, hasn't it? But being a 'thrifter', is a different thing altogether. It rhymes with drifter and glitter and sounds vaguely romantic or slightly bohemian; don't you just love it already? Okay, so you may not be familiar with the word thrifter, but be assured that in six months' time you won't know how you lived without it.

Thrifting is all about the pleasure of second-hand clothes and getting beautiful things on the cheap. It's about cherishing and taking care of what you own.

The generation who lived through the Second World War took on thrift as a necessity. For them, utility wear and rationing was a part of everyday life. The inter-war 'make do and mend' years decreed that wearing full skirts – or indeed anything that required an extravagant amount of fabric – was tantamount to treason.

My granny, who was a fashion designer in the 1940s, spent much of her time 'turning coats'. For those of you who don't know what that means, let me explain it. People would pay her to remake their winter coats by turning them inside out, so that the fabric appeared fresh and they could get another year out of that one garment.

I know this may seem a little barmy to the generations who know nothing of rations and have never experienced mass unemployment, but there was a time, before the boom, when people really cherished their belongings – they had to. Now, I'm not suggesting that you learn to darn socks, sew patches on your Chanel or turn your coat inside out, but I am suggesting that you start to look at things a little differently.

41

It's no longer about being able to afford a Preen jacket or a Prada handbag. Thrift is about enjoying what you've got and keeping it at its peak. It's about, in *Vogue*'s words, 'making use of what we own'. So look away from the catwalk, ladies, because it's time to shop for clothes that will stand the test of time rather than the fast fashion we've all come to love.

Stop buying so much throwaway fashion that falls apart after just a few washes; buy a single great investment piece – coat, boots or bag – something incredible that you can keep for a number of years. Once you have a few great high-quality basics, your wardrobe will work that much harder for you.

## Gucci? No, Darling, It's Oxfam

Buying in thrift stores has lost its stigma; even style icons such as Kate Moss, Madonna and Sienna Miller love the second-hand look. So isn't it time you learnt to love it too?

Suddenly second hand need not mean second best. Indeed, second-hand clothes are enjoying a bit of a renaissance at the moment. From Oxfam to Enable Ireland or War on Want, your local thrift store offers a plethora of bargains. Regardless of the trends of the moment, second-hand shops will always be there to provide an alternative.

One of my favourite haunts is Oxfam on Dublin's Georges Street. In the last few years the quality of goods has improved considerably. Recent finds in the Georges Street shop include Chloé blouses, Armani suits, a Marni belt and Hermès scarves. The shop also stocks an incredible selection of designer bridal gowns and evening wear in their upstairs salon, with plenty on offer to tempt shoppers. There's a thrift store on nearly every Irish high street, so pop down for a rummage because you never know what gems you may come across. More than anything else, I love the thrill of the hunt and rifling through the rails, because you just never know what you will uncover. Just enjoy thrifting for the wonderful time-wasting activity it can be – a break from chores and a couple of hours spent mooching about. Here are a few tips for finding the best buys:

*Tailor made*

If you find a great dress but it's too big, worry not. Snap it up at a bargain price and take it to a tailor who can alter it. You'll still save.

*Designer labels*

You can find fabulous designer pieces but you have to expect higher prices. For high-end labels, head to charity shops in upmarket areas.

*Check the stress points*

If clothes are going to give out too soon, it's likely going to be at the stress points – elbows, underarms, etc. So check to make sure they can withstand another wearing.

*Run zippers up and down to ensure they work*

Check to make sure buttons are intact and snaps work. If the zipper is broken ask for a discount.

*Clean them*

It's always a great idea to run the clothes through the laundry before adding them to your closet. While the clothes that you buy should be clean, it never hurts to be on the safe side.

**Customise It**

Shopping second hand is not the only option when times get hard and you don't want to compromise on style. If your budget doesn't quite stretch to a new dress, there's plenty you can do to inject some glamour into your current wardrobe. With a little creativity and the right materials, customising an outfit is the ideal way to economise and give your closet a little 'oomph!' at the same time.

Stick or sew beads or sequins on to a dress – an easy way to add a dash of glamour – or add a glittery, sequined trim, either by hand or machine. Trimmings are all the rage at the moment – with feathers in particular tickling my fancy. A boring black evening dress can be transformed by adding a dramatic feathered trim to the hem or neckline. For a really quick fix, you can use Wonderweb and iron it on.

Customising is a unique and original way to express your personality too. Sarah Jessica Parker, whose style is universally applauded, reigns as queen of the customised mix 'n' match. While her closet may be filled with expensive designer labels, it's not difficult to imagine her complementing her whimsical look with an unusual accessory from a second-hand or haberdashery shop, be it a flower tucked in her hair, a ribbon belt or a handbag with an unusual beaded detail.

Depending on my mood, I usually find inspiration by wandering into my nearest haberdashery or vintage shop. All those flowers, glitter and sparkle always get my creative juices flowing. Take a boring jacket or a T-shirt and you can give it a funky new look by decorating it with lace, ribbon or a corsage, or even a heat transfer (which you can stick on by using an iron).

Something as simple as changing the buttons on an inexpensive coat can help transform a bargain buy into something really special. For instance, adding a colourful ribbon to a plain dress or cardigan will immediately make it appear more fashion forward.

If you have a dress that is a really great shape on you but you've tired of the colour, why not dye it? A summer dress can work for winter too if you dye it a darker shade, such as aubergine, navy or jade. Old evening dresses can also be given a second lease of life by cutting them into dazzling tops, which work best teamed with jeans and some strappy heels.

Be it dyeing, cutting, adding or subtracting, you'd be surprised what a few minor alterations can do to bring your dreary duds right up to date.

### Three top customising tips

Change it. Change the buttons on your garments, either by using buttons from other garments that you no longer wear, or picking them up from charity shops. Other changes can involve:

### Ribbons

Ribbons of all lengths, widths and colours are very useful when customising a dull outfit. Plain, tailored shirts can be brightened up with a thick ribbon belt tied slightly to the side on the front.

### Jewellery

If you've been housing the same costume items in your jewellery box for years, why not brighten up a garment and give old jewellery a new purpose? Try attaching glittery brooches to a beret or onto fabric handbags for a touch of hippy sparkle.

Trimmings

Find your local haberdashery store and pick out some beautiful ribbon, beads, faux-fur trimmings or feathers – they can transform any item of clothing.

## Swap 'til You Drop

Still not convinced? Try a clothes-swap party and you'll soon discover that swapping is the new shopping.

We all know the scenario: you spot something like a cerise puffball skirt looking impossibly fabulous in the pages of *Vogue*. Five minutes later, you decide that your life would be infinitely better if you were in possession of such a glorious garment. Then, gripped with what can only be described as some sort of low-level mental illness, you dash into town to buy the object of your desire.

It's only when you get home and try the damn thing on that you realise it doesn't suit you; that's when you remember the wallet-numbing price tag.

From bum bags to batwing sleeves, moonboots, culottes, snoods – we have all bought really *bad* fashion at some point in our lives. Indeed, the impulse buy is something that many of us ladies are, sadly, all too familiar with. But is it possible to rid ourselves of our sartorial sins? Are you looking to offload some old clothes and maybe gain some new ones? If so, why not throw a clothes swap party?

Swap parties are a great excuse for a girlie get-together to which you can bring shoes, jewellery and accessories as well as clothes you no longer wear – or like. The idea that you can end up with a completely free wardrobe, while disposing of those instantly regretted purchases (which seemed like a good idea at the time) is, quite frankly, a dizzying prospect. Invite a group of friends around, asking each of them to bring tasteful and stylish items to swap.

Throw in refreshments and giggle your way to a free wardrobe fix.

Bring at least five items – they must be in good nick – but you can leave with as many as you manage to bag. Make sure they're clean and ironed (it's seriously rude to turn up with creased rags and expect to walk away with a barely worn Marc Jacobs blouse). The hostess provides a clothes rail on which everything is hung, giving guests a happy hour or so to look through the swag.

You can't actually claim any items during this time (patience, patience!). A five-minute warning should be announced before 'go', but as soon as the 'swap' is declared open, guests can grab what they want (no biting, scratching or elbowing allowed). Five minutes later you might be the proud new owner of a friend's too-small Gina shoes or a great D&G jacket that somebody just got tired of.

*Hints and tips for successful swapping*

Invitations

It's best to invite around ten people – any more and you will be playing referee in a living-room floor scuffle over the pink prom dress that everyone has their eye on.

Sizes

Do make sure that there's a balance in sizes. You don't want a lonely size 8 or a curvy size 16 to spend the evening alone with no-one to swap with.

Makeshift clothes rails

On the day of the party make sure you have designated areas for tops, bottoms and dresses. If you don't have a wardrobe rack, get creative with the space and furniture you do have.

Changing space

Be sure to provide a private place to try on clothes for the more modest of your guests, as well as several mirrors in different places to avoid traffic jams.

## Find a New Wardrobe with the Click of a Mouse

Why not join the legions of fashion fans who shop almost exclusively on eBay? When someone asks you where you got your fabulous new jacket, the smuggest reply is no longer 'Topshop'. These days, the truly savvy shopper gets her best bargains on eBay. The website www.ebay.com has been around since 1995 and has an estimated 95 millions users worldwide; it's a great place to find designer labels and all sorts – on the cheap.

If you have never shopped on eBay, you have an exciting experience awaiting you. You will be amazed at what can be found, but we will concentrate on clothing for now. There are several ways to find what you are looking for. I find the easiest way is to first go to the Clothing, Shoes and Accessories area. From there you may type in what you are looking for and this will then bring up an impressive list of items, which you then bid on.

The most expensive item I have ever bought on eBay was a Diane von Furstenberg wrap dress at €250, but it was still a fraction of the cost of a new one. You can sell literally anything and buy literally anything – from a yucky fake gold signet ring for €1 (why bother?) to a crocodile Hermès Birkin bag for €57,900 (a steal!).

Shopping on eBay isn't a hobby – it's a competitive sport. Auctions can last for seven days and a battle of wills develops, as women all over the world stare at their computers – women with narrow-eyed determination – waiting until the bitter end. It's the winning that counts.

Then the tortuous wait for the postman begins. Sometimes you can click the 'buy it now' button, which is when the seller asks for a price and you agree to pay it. This means you don't have to go through the whole auction, which can end in tears.

As a seasoned eBay shopper – and seller – here's a few tips. Antique jewellery is ridiculously cheap on eBay so forget about going to any of those overpriced vintage stores because you can get real gems and rhinestones online for a song. Vintage clothes are surprisingly affordable and you can also come across some well-known designer labels at a fraction of the shop price.

Although the bargains are myriad, it's worth exercising some caution. Some of the designer handbags will be more Canal Street than Brown Thomas. So ensure your purchase comes with a certificate of authenticity, which all real designer handbags include. Using eBay is not only a savvy way to shop – it's great fun as well. (For more details, go to www.ebay.ie.)

**Time to Change Your Shopping Habits – for Good**

Yes, 'recession' may be the word that's on everyone's lips at the minute. But a financial slump is no excuse for turning into a fashion frump, darling!

So, have I convinced you? Are you ready to join the growing band of recessionistas who always manage to look stylish despite the credit crunch? Are you ready to change your shopping habits by going with the grain of the recession, of making do and mending? Are you going to keep perfectly good clothes, even when the fashion roundabout has moved on? Are you going to save up to buy things?

Now you can look fashionable this season without abusing the environment, oppressing the poor or breaking your increasingly stretched budget. Thrift is smart. It's about individual glamour, and being original and truly stylish without spending thousands on current fashion.

And that has to be a good thing.

# 5

# Home Improvements:
# Decorating in a Downturn

## Eoin Lyons

Now is a time when we all need some cheer, and one of the best ways to bring some joy into your life is to create a home that makes you feel good. Everyone knows that being in a nice environment has a positive effect on one's mood.

The spirit of the moment is to renovate rather than relocate, by improving what you already have. In theory, everyone can create a home that looks and feels good. Even on a budget.

### Number Crunch

Stamp duty is one very good financial reason to 'sit tight' and make the most out of your current home, rather than submit to the stress of moving house. The stamp duty on a house with a price tag of **€350,000** – the average house price in Dublin at the end of 2008 – will arrive at a tax bill of **€15,750** (under the rules in place as of February 2009). Think how many new armchairs, bathroom tiles and kitchen cabinets you could buy for that sum!

Decorating your home isn't something you have to do in one fell swoop or with an open chequebook. First decide which changes will make the greatest impact quickly and bring you the most pleasure, and which jobs can wait a while. List projects that you can accomplish in a day or a week or a month, and those that will take longer.

**Mix and Match**

There are now a great many excellent interior sources around the country, from mass-market to speciality stores, so shop around. Mixing things from inexpensive chain stores and small expensive shops is the way to go.

Diversify your shopping: go to department stores and low-end retail outlets to take advantage of the best each has to offer. Don't overlook charity shops as you never know what you'll find. Start going to auctions – they're fun and good value.

**Use Natural Elements**

The way you style or dress a room makes a big difference and can cost very little. Bringing the outdoors inside is one of the easiest and most affordable ways to create a pleasant atmosphere. A simple vase of flowers or a basket of roughly chopped logs makes a home so much more cheerful.

Collect natural memories. From holidays, bring back shells, rocks, pinecones – anything that will act as a reminder of your travels. An old piece of wood can be used as a dining-table centrepiece or shells used to separate objects on a bookcase.

Bringing nature indoors doesn't necessarily mean spending a lot in a florist's shop. Greenery from the garden, bunched together in a clear glass container, has a sculptural quality. Always keep things unpretentious and stay away from contrived bouquets. Ivy is great in winter – use great big swathes of it tumbling out of a vase.

## Small Luxuries Matter

You can make your home special without spending a fortune. Small luxuries can have a big impact on how the place feels. Good-quality sheets, goose down pillows and fine soaps won't hide that worn carpet or the wall that needs to be painted, but they will make you feel pampered. Small things matter. Wait for the sales and buy the best you can, one good item at a time. Scented candles and tea lights should be an everyday treat. Light them when you come home after a hard day and you might just feel a little better.

## Hang Art

Art always enhances your home. I don't mean a painting with a five-figure price tag. From treasured items, such as children's artwork or family photographs, to pages taken from an art book, have beautiful things on your walls. Frames are all-important. Chain stores do decent simple ones cheaply, but auction rooms often have old (but not particularly valuable) frames that can be picked up for relatively little. Think too about how your pictures are hung. Create an arrangement that's pleasing and balanced as it will make a big difference to a room and, again, costs little to achieve.

## Declutter

Decluttering will make a big impact. Apart from a bottle or two of Cif, this approach is cost free. Set aside a weekend to do things such as vacuuming the top of curtains, washing light fittings, shampooing carpets, wiping paint-work and so on. Rope in a few friends – you can always repay them with a good dinner at the end of a day's work. Get rid of as much old paraphernalia as possible. Rooms will look bigger and brighter.

Decluttering does not mean living in a super-minimal way and is as much about organisation as anything else. A home can have only so much broken crockery, odd cutlery and old appliances – all these should go. Also think about the way you display things. Perhaps the hearth of a fireplace could be used to hold a collection of simple glass jars and vases. Everyday objects can be beautiful if grouped together.

### Start Painting

Painting your walls is the fastest and cheapest way to make a major change. Personally I think walls (and curtains) should be relatively neutral, whether dark or light in colour, to allow interesting furniture, art and objects to take centre stage.

When choosing a paint colour, the best way to do it is to paint a large 4-foot by 8-foot board with a sample of the shade you're considering. Live with it for a few days and see how you feel. Colour changes depending on the light, so note how it looks at different times of the day. The putty shade that looked good in the paint shop could look grim on your walls.

If you can get a professional to do your painting, it's worth it in the long run. But that's a luxury. If you choose to do the painting yourself, use quality materials – paint, brushes and rollers. They will help you to get the job done faster and give a better finish. Buying cheap paint is a false economy. It won't give good coverage and could look patchy. A bad brush makes applying the paint much more laborious.

Prep your walls and woodwork before you start. That means washing them down, filling in any holes and sanding so you have a smooth surface. Make sure you remove the dust created by sanding. Tape over light switches and remove fittings, if possible, before applying a coat of primer. Paint the ceiling first and then start at the top of the walls and work down. Allow the paint to dry between coats and apply at least two top coats.

## First Impressions

The entrance hall is the introduction to the rest of your home, a buffer between you and the outside world. Most people put decorating other parts of the house before their hall. It is nevertheless the first part of your home that you and your visitors step into and the last part that you leave.

A warm, welcoming, pleasant hall is good to come home to and is less depressing after a hard day than opening the hall door to a dark, dull space strewn with schoolbags, sports equipment and shoes. Obviously when you budget the cost of redecorating your home, you have to allow most money for the rooms you are actually going to live in. But once you have decided on that, it's time to turn your thought and care – if not a little money – to making your hall as warm, welcoming and practical as you can.

Theoretically, halls should be inexpensive to decorate as there is little to purchase in the way of furniture, unless you are blessed with a wide and spacious area. Country halls look well in materials such as quarry tiles, flagstones, slate or brick. If you are laying these from scratch, lay underfloor heating. It is not terribly expensive, should be easy for your builder to do and makes a world of difference.

If for some reason you cannot have tiles, keep your bare boards sanded and sealed. Paint the boards with special hard-wearing paint if they are in bad condition and you cannot afford to lay a new wood floor. Elegance and economy aren't natural enemies in the hall: enhance the sense of light with a wall of mirrors. To achieve this glamorous feature, use mirrored tiles, available in different sizes from most big DIY stores. They can be grouted and attached to the wall. Sometimes a long, low table is better than one at a regular height and makes a narrow hallway seem just a little more airy.

**Living Large**

The key to decorating a living room is to think simple. One good-sized sofa plus as many different occasional chairs is better than a formal arrangement. Let the room have personality: it's a place for displaying collections or beautiful objects. The point of the living room is to be a space to enjoy yourself in, but comfort shouldn't cancel out style. Keep things uncluttered, yet interesting.

A sofa is one of the largest and potentially most expensive items you'll buy for your home, so, if decorating a living room from scratch, buy the sofa first as it will determine the scale of all your other furnishings. Regardless of the price range – whether you're buying a sofa from a shop floor or having one specially made – always have the dimensions of your room to hand when you shop. Avoid buying a very cheap sofa: it will almost certainly look shabby fast. But neither do you need to spend a fortune: the middle market is very well served when it comes to sofas.

The easiest way to test the quality of a sofa is to see if the fabric creases when you sit on it or if the sofa fails to bounce back to its original shape when you stand up.

Top-quality sofas offer the most resistance because, whether filled with feathers or foam, they are the most tightly packed. Make sure you can remove the sofa covers for cleaning.

In general, when buying a large piece of furniture such as a sofa, measure its dimensions when in the shop and recreate the size at home using newspapers. It will give you an idea of how the piece will fit into your room and could save on expensive mistakes.

A patterned cushion is a lot less risky (and a lot less permanent) than a pair of armchairs in a wild fabric. Think about keeping major pieces of upholstered furniture neutral. Sofas are an investment and you'll want yours to stick around for many years.

A throw adds a contrasting colour and extra texture to a sofa. When folded across the arm, it's ready for use as an aid to getting cosy. Or use a large one spread across the seat and back of the sofa for an instant change of look. A patterned throw brings instant personality to a plain sofa. A similar effect could be achieved by buying a yard-and-a-half of fabric and laying it over the sofa in the same way. This need not look student-flat-y: fabric shops often sell off odd pieces of expensive fabrics at bargain prices and these are perfect for this sort of thing.

For a fast change, think about using your existing furniture in a different way. Take one piece out and see what space is created. Re-arrange what you have: put the sofa in a different position or put a side-table between two armchairs, anything that shakes things up.

### Dine In Style

If you do not have the luxury of a dining room used just for dining – and most of us do not – the trick is to make your dining table look as if it's not a dining table most of the time. This means not having a table surrounded by chairs – except, of course, when you are actually going to use it for eating. The problem of where to put those extra chairs is not really so very difficult to resolve. You could buy chairs that act as occasional chairs; they can be distributed throughout bedrooms and the hall, if it is big enough, and then brought together when needed.

These days you do not have to go for matching suites of dining furniture. No one will look askance if you have a makeshift table disguised by a floor-length tablecloth, painted or lacquered ex-kitchen chairs and a Victorian wardrobe for glass and china storage. Why should they? What you are achieving with such a happy mix is much more personal and therefore more interesting than the blandness of the careful match.

If you can't afford a good antique table, get a second-hand junk table and do what you can with it: paint it, strip it or cover it with cloth. Then invest as much as you can in comfortable chairs. You can still achieve a traditional feeling without having to spend a lot of money on antique chairs. Not particularly nice reproduction chairs can be lacquered in unexpected colours. And so on. Antique furniture gets a great face-lift just by being set against a clean backdrop.

**Kitchen Tips**

The marketplace is overflowing with kitchen units that answer every style idea and price point, but the best approach is to keep it simple. A good recipe is clean, pale Shaker-style cabinets, a splashback of white rectangular tiles, pale marble countertops and stainless-steel appliances for contrast. Choose small nickel knobs or handles that are unobtrusive. It is not a good idea to decorate a kitchen around a theme: you don't live in Provence, so don't do a Provençal kitchen.

If your budget doesn't stretch to a whole new kitchen, you can update your existing one by buying new appliances if you can, retiling the splashback or painting the walls. Refresh a tired sink with new taps. Paint the inside of glass-fronted cabinets. Revive a wood floor with super-durable enamel outdoor paint.

Existing kitchen units can be given a face-lift without the expense of replacing them entirely. Handles can be changed and new doors can be put on the old carcasses, or old doors can be removed, sanded down and then painted and varnished. If the surfaces are laminate, you will need to use a specialist paint or primer. Talk to a joiner about possibilities.

Generally, although natural stone countertops can be expensive, they're worth the investment in terms of beauty and durability. Rubber or resin floors are soft underfoot, durable and available in almost any colour. Kitchen floors need to be tough enough to withstand spills, grease and damp, but comfortable to stand on for long periods and handsome to look at.

Old pieces of furniture can be given a new lease of life in a kitchen. Re-utilising materials is a way of saving money and creating something that's unique. Painting everything white has a unifying effect. Stainless steel appliances lend a sense of modernity.

**Sleep Easy**

Your bedroom should be about comfort and beauty. It's the space you wake up in and the last place you see before the end of the day. Serenity is key, so paint the walls pale, calm shades. White can be bleak so choose a white with a pink tint.

Choose a really good bed, be it a divan or a mattress that sits in a frame. Restful sleep is impossible on a bed that is lumpy, uncomfortable or too small, so it is worth spending a little money and economising on everything else. If you haven't bought a new bed in ten years, it's time to update. Look for a bed with layers of small nests of memory foam as these respond better to the shape of your body.

**Bathroom Bliss**

Bathroom makeovers don't need to be as difficult – or as expensive – as you might imagine. It's possible to make a few small changes, such as adding new taps or a sink, or doing a paint job or redoing the tiles, that will – without spending a lot of money – give the room a new feeling. First take stock of what you need to do. Do you want to recreate the luxury feel of a spa or have something more simple? And, of course, how much can you afford to spend?

There are so many styles, fixtures and materials out there that it helps to have an idea of what you want before you start looking. While staying open to new ideas, stick with your own priorities.

There's nothing wrong with opting for an inexpensive tile – and you don't need to go bananas on the latest gimmick. Instead, put money into the sink, bath, toilet and shower. In my opinion, bathrooms should be as light, bright and airy as possible. Never choose anything other than white sanitary ware.

Start by visiting bathroom showrooms to find ideas, then look at your own space and think about what works and what doesn't. Maybe some fittings can be retained and smartened up. Consult your plumber or builder early on to identify any limitations and avoid mistakes that will cost money to correct. If you are redoing your floor it's very easy to have underfloor heating laid under a stone or tile floor. It makes such a difference to the comfort of the room and can be linked to the regular heating system in the rest of the house.

Now that staying in is the new going out, and doing up has replaced trading up, feathering your nest makes more sense than ever. And with previously elusive tradesmen and overpriced furniture emporiums forced to become increasingly competitive, it's also a whole lot more affordable.

# CRUNCH-PROOFING YOUR LIFESTYLE

# 6

# From Slim Pickings to Self-Sufficiency: Growing Your Own Food

**Michael Kelly**

At times of crisis, when my sense of perspective is in need of realignment, I find solace in the vegetable plot here on our windswept acre in rural Waterford. Tragic US poet Sara Teasdale wrote a poem in the 1920s called 'There Will Come Soft Rain' in which she reminds us that, no matter how important we think we are or how serious we think our troubles have become, Mother Nature is basically ignoring us and doing her own thing. In fact, Teasdale argued that if mankind was to be wiped off the face of the earth in the morning, 'And Spring herself, when she woke at dawn / Would scarcely know that we were gone.' Strangely, I always find immense comfort in that sentiment.

I'm not the kind of person who has a relevant quote from a poem on hand for every occasion, but Teasdale's wonderful verse came to mind one morning in late 2008 as I was outside in the garden picking carrots to go into a nice hearty stew for that night's dinner. After listening to an hour's worth of bad news on *Morning Ireland* about the global economy, I was feeling tetchy and irritable and all of a sudden I got a peculiar desire to cook a stew. I don't know where this came from, but deep down I think something as nebulous as a global economic crisis just makes you want to get in touch with things that are real. Like a stew, for example (bear with me, this is going somewhere).

I switched off the news, put on my wellies and went outside the back door to have a root around in the vegetable plot. The sun was shining and there was a vague hint of a frost on the grass. Birds were singing, cobwebs were glistening with moisture, the dogs were trying to warm themselves up on the corner of the deck and our ever-expanding flock of hens were preening themselves in front of the kitchen window. It was a beautiful, crisp winter morning when everything seemed possible.

Even at that time of the year, when the pickings in the garden were slim, there was enough available to keep the stew pot happy. Crazy-shaped, intensely sweet carrots and juicy stalks of celery were plucked from the ground; onions and generous handfuls of fresh thyme and parsley were collected from the polytunnel; from the freezer came a home-made stock and (best of all) some gigot lamb chops (the result of a fruitful pork-for-lamb bartering arrangement with a neighbour).

In no time at all, the smell of the stew filled the house and all seemed right with the world again. And you know why? Mother Nature doesn't give two hoots about a recession or banking crisis. She doesn't give it a thought. She knows nothing of multi-billion dollar bailouts of the world's banking system. She knows nothing of *Sky News* 'Alerts' or interest-rate hikes, or of the US Fed, liquidity, capitalisation or short selling. She cares nothing at all for bankers or traders or fat cats (except the feline variety). She would never concern herself with such grubbiness.

Instead, she busies herself making those crazy-shaped carrots grow, gently urging the sun to shine to warm the hens' backs or concocting that restorative frost to break down the soil after a busy growing season. She busies herself marshalling the relentless cycle of the seasons – from the excited anticipation of spring through the boundless potential of summer, the conviviality and abundance of the autumn harvest, and finally the gentle, melancholic pause of winter. Amidst all the gloom and doom, boom and bust, allow yourself to be consoled with the thought that Mother Nature couldn't care less about the recession. There will come soft rain.

I've been writing about producing your own food for about four years now and thinking about it even longer. On a number of occasions I've heard people pooh-poohing the idea of self-sufficiency, and dismissing it as a hobby for upper-middle-class toffs with too much time on their hands. But around the time that the vet was called to put down the poor old Celtic Tiger, a broader group of people started getting interested in a return to the simple pleasures of 'the good life'.

I'm inclined to think that the reasons for this are more complex than a straightforward desire to save a few bob at the checkout. I think a lot of it comes down to the general sense of unease that follows when institutions we have come to rely on and consider central to society start to fail. If banks and airlines are dropping like flies, then what about supermarkets and food suppliers? If jobs, incomes and homes are at risk, will we be able to feed ourselves in the long term?

At times like these, when the very fabric of our society seems under threat, people start to worry about really fundamental things – and food security is the most fundamental thing of all. When you add to that the concerns that most of us have had for years about food quality, miles and ethics, and the impact of the food system on our environment, you have a really powerful motivation to grow your own. It may be overstating it a little to say that growing your own has become necessary, but at least we can say that it now seems to makes perfect sense. In particular, it makes financial sense.

There's sweet bugger all that any of us can do about some of the problems we face in the world today – climate change, economic woes, etc. – and as a result of being so totally powerless, it's easy to feel completely overwhelmed. Psychiatrists say that during times of economic recession, greater numbers of people suffer from insomnia, anxiety and depression, and, worst of all, suicide rates creep up.

I'm not going to say that sticking a fork in the soil is going to make all your worries vamoose (though getting out in the fresh air, getting some exercise and interacting with living things will almost certainly help), but think about it this way: of all the things that you are powerless about, food security is not one of them. That's the beauty of producing your own food – it's incredibly proactive. You can do it right now if you want (maybe finish this chapter first), or later today or tomorrow or at the weekend. Just stick a seed in the ground and watch it grow. And don't worry if you don't know much about growing things because here's a little secret I will let you in on: things want to grow. When you stick a seed in the soil it will generally thrive, despite your best efforts to prevent it from doing so by planting it in the wrong type of soil, at the wrong time of the year or upside-down.

Growing your own is not the preserve of any one social class. It's not the preserve of country people or city people. It's accessible to anyone with the motivation and access to even the smallest patch of ground. In the clamour for allotments, people often neglect the potential veg-growing asset that's waiting for them outside their back door (presently covered in dumb lawn), usually on the grounds that it's too small. I wrote a piece about 'urban farmers' last year in which I profiled four people with small (sometimes tiny) city gardens who are almost self-sufficient. They grow all manner of fruit and vegetables, and in some cases rear animals for the table.

Our cities and towns have a tremendous tradition of urban farming and residents of a certain age will no doubt recall a time when allotments, cow yards, dairies and pig farms were a prominent feature of urban life. Over the last three or four decades, however, as our affluence has increased, we've changed our views on what back gardens are actually for – instead of seeing them as an asset that can be put to work, we see them as outdoor entertainment venues. Your back garden, no matter how small (hell, even your balcony) has the potential to become Food Production Central and save you money at the same time.

Can you really become self-sufficient and save yourself a heap of money by growing your own vegetables? Yes and Yes. But here's an important point – you don't have to be 100 per cent self-sufficient for it to be worthwhile. When I go to the supermarket I still get a kick out of the fact that I can walk right by the shelf where they keep the onions, for example (we haven't had to buy an onion in years), and that wonderful feeling of self-satisfied smugness is not diminished in any way by the fact that there are other things that I do have to buy. Do I feel bad when our own spuds run out after three or four blissful months of enjoying the floury marvels and we have to start eating shop-bought ones again? Yes. Does it make my spud growing enterprise pointless? Absolutely not. Any move (no matter how small) towards self-sufficiency is incredibly worthwhile.

Each year, as we grow more and manage to screw up less, there are increased savings at the checkout. There are some things that we rarely need to buy at all anymore. I can't tell you the last time we bought any of the following, for example: eggs, onions, garlic, celery, strawberries, raspberries, apples, herbs, pork or bacon – the list goes on. From late spring through to late autumn, when the vegetable plot is at its most generous and the larder is full, we are more or less completely self-sufficient in meat, fruit and vegetables. Our trips to the supermarket are rare and when we do darken the door, because we are only buying things we can't produce ourselves (flour, pasta, milk, oil, etc.), our bill is a fraction of what it would otherwise be.

There is a bountiful supply from the garden of all the really useful vegetables that you need for sauces, stocks and soups – potatoes, garlic, carrots, leeks, celery, shallots and onions. Those out-of-vogue vegetables that your mother told you to eat up (and stop complaining about it) – turnip, cauliflower and cabbage, for example – are pretty easy to grow too. During that time of the year that we Irish euphemistically call 'summer' there are peas and beans, courgettes, radishes, rocket, lettuces, tomatoes, cucumbers, beets and kohlrabies. Later in the autumn, we get squashes, pumpkins, red cabbage, peppers, aubergines and celeriac. Even in the grim bareness of winter there are some greens doing their best to keep our antioxidant levels up and colds and flus at bay – brussels sprouts, perpetual spinach, chard, kale and winter salads. Our tentative forays into keeping pigs and chickens for the table means that, for six or seven months of the year, there is a freezer full of the best free-range meat imaginable.

Even if you don't have much space or expertise, there are some things that take up very little space (they will do well in pots on a balcony, for example) and will save you a small fortune. Take herbs as an example. All the main herbs that you need to transform a dreary dish into a culinary opus – basil, chives, parsley, thyme, mint, rosemary, marjoram – are voracious growers. Your main problem will be preventing them from taking over the joint. You can walk outside your back door and pull enormous handfuls of the stuff as required. Contrast that with those miserable little packets of herbs, often of questionable quality, that you buy for €3 each – the ones that frequently end up rotting at the back of your fridge.

And these are just the things that you can produce in your own garden. Let's not forget the 'free' food that Mother Nature makes available in the rivers and seas, fields, forests and ditches. Some of the finest produce imaginable is just sitting there waiting to be pilfered (or is running or swimming away from you at speed) – mackerels, rabbits, berries, elderflowers, etc. – and somehow tastes even better because it is completely and totally free.

As more and more people get involved in producing their own food, there are also new opportunities for bartering and exchanging produce. We joined a network in Waterford last year for people who grow their own food, where the swapping of produce is encouraged (and of course the swapping of ideas, suggestions, tips and war-stories). The fact that nearly a hundred people showed up at the first meeting of that network is further proof, if it is required, of just how much interest there is out there in self-sufficiency and all its facets.

### Number Crunch

If you baulk at the idea of growing your own, you can always opt to support people who do: there are around **140 farmers' markets** in Ireland, according to Bord Bia. Meanwhile, the market for organic food in Ireland is estimated to be worth more than **€100 million**, while despite our best efforts to live on a diet of toast and chocolate, total sales of fresh fruit and vegetables in retail outlets had reached **€1.2 billion** by 2007.

In the interests of fairness, I should of course mention that not all our attempts at food production are a resounding success (mostly due to our chronic lack of knowledge). As I mentioned, instead of being long and smooth, our carrots are stubby and forked, like some strange aliens or prehistoric life-forms. Sometimes our potatoes get blight, rocket goes to seed or some of our garlic crop rots in the ground. We have lost some crops to the lowly garden slug and others to our nemesis, the rabbit. Pigs have escaped, hens have stopped laying and we have reared some chickens that had about as much meat on them as a Pygmy shrew. Sometimes we fall victim to our failures, other times to our successes – last year, for example, we had a never-ending glut of blindingly hot and practically inedible giant red mustard leaf (pass the Kleenex please).

Still, we stumble along with blind enthusiasm for the project. Some of the most memorable and downright honest moments of my whole life have taken place in the little piece of heaven that is our vegetable garden: up to my neck in muck and dirt after spending an entire day barrowing tonnes of manure onto our raised beds; satisfyingly painful limbs after a day spent digging and weeding; the joy of the first pea or strawberry of summer; the sight of a warm egg on a bed of straw or the crowing of Roger the feisty cockerel at first light; working in the weatherproof polytunnel with the rain pounding on the plastic overhead; and going off to collect two wriggling, squealing piglets at Easter.

Producing your own food is undoubtedly one of the most practical things you can do to take the edge off the recession, but it is the non-financial rewards – the profoundly real moments described above – that will keep you coming back long after the Irish economy has pulled itself from the morass it currently languishes in.

# 7

# In Praise of Bangernomics: Driving for Less

**Kilian Doyle**

Assuming you don't have a collection of Picassos in your kitchen or a predilection for clothes made of silk-thin sheets of platinum adorned with Dodo feathers, the car you buy will be the second most expensive purchase of your life after your house.

It used to be that driving a new car was a way of telling everyone else you'd made it. Times change. Nowadays it's a way of telling them you're probably up to your oxters in debt.

I'm assuming that the fact you are reading this book at all means you are not the type of profligate head case who splashes out on a brand new motor. (If you are, what are you doing here? Scoffing at us scrimpers? Haven't you something better to be doing? Like flushing diamonds down a toilet somewhere?)

In these straitened times, only drug dealers, lottery winners, lunatics and benefit-in-kind beneficiaries buy new cars. For the normal motorist buying a car with their own money, buying a new car is the worst investment you can make (unless you've sunk all your life savings into buying Icelandic bank shares). The simple rule, if you want to save money, is that you just don't do it. Ever.

## Number Crunch

Playing the 'spot the new registration' game is a lot harder when new car sales are falling by **66 per cent**, as they did in Ireland between 2008 and 2009. Some **15,929 new cars** were sold in January 2009, compared to **47,609** in January 2008, as consumer spending on discretionary, big-ticket items dried up during what is usually the busiest time of year for the car industry. Layoffs at car dealerships and car parts firms based in Ireland swiftly ensued.

Depreciation, as we all know, is the thief of cash. The simple fact is this – once you've driven it off the lot, the average new car depreciates as quickly as a Boeing 747 plummeting towards the sea after its wings have fallen off mid-flight.

Alright, so that's a slight exaggeration, but, while it depends on the model, a car really can lose 20 per cent of its value the second you stick the key in the ignition for the first time. What's more, it'll be worth half of what you paid within five short years. You may as well set fire to a big pile of banknotes on your driveway as put a brand new car on it. It'll have the same effect on your bank balance.

So the sensible thing to do is – it goes without saying – to buy second-hand. If you are concerned about warranties and new technology, that's no problem. Just go nearly-new. You'll still be paying 20 per cent less even if the car is only a few months old.

There was a time when, without hesitation, I would have advised anyone thinking of buying a nearly-new used car to go to the UK. Even factoring in the price of Vehicle Registration Tax (VRT) and cost of ferries et al., you could save thousands on sourcing a car. But times have changed. Irish used-car lots are packed full of cars that aren't shifting. There is currently way more supply than demand and, as a result, there are incredible bargains to be had on forecourts.

The Society of the Irish Motor Industry (SIMI) reported late last year that prices had dropped by over 20 per cent in 2008 as dealers desperately tried to offload all their unsold stock. There are a lot of reasons for the glut, not least the new $CO_2$-based road tax system, which makes buying a new low-emissions car more attractive. (This seems to me to be extreme folly. You'd have to be saving thousands of euro in road tax a year – rather than hundreds – to make taking the depreciation hit on a new car worthwhile. However, if you are doing it for ecological rather than financial reasons, good for you. Would that we all were in such a position.)

Another reason for the huge amount of used cars available is the increase in repossessed vehicles being returned by finance companies, as consumers struggle to meet repayments. As a result, auctions are flourishing as financiers try to offload these cars to recoup their losses. So someone's loss can be your gain. (If you have any qualms about profiting from the previous owner's misfortune, think of it this way: if they hadn't been spending someone else's cash like a drunken sailor, they wouldn't be out of their financial depth and car-less now, would they?)

Don't be afraid to try your luck at an auction. They're no longer just for fat blokes in sheepskin coats. In some large auction houses, private buyers account for up to 40 per cent of customers, up from less than 6 per cent five years ago. In most auctions, prospective buyers are free to inspect cars beforehand with mechanics and even view engineers' reports on the vehicles. Not only that, but the majority of the cars that have been repossessed are under warranty, so even if you are unlucky enough to buy a lemon, you have some comeback.

The best advice if you are thinking of buying at auction but are a bit nervous about making a fool of yourself or buying a clunker, is to go to a few to see how they operate before you start bidding yourself. You'll soon realise that the process is professionally handled and there's no danger of ending up with a bill for a Lamborghini because the auctioneer mistook your facial tic for a sneaky bid.

Once you've decided on the type of car you want, do a bit of research. Take the price a similar model is being sold for at a dealership, knock 20 per cent off that and set the resulting total as your maximum. Don't bid above it. It's easy to get carried away, but there's no need. With the glut of cars on the market there will always be another one.

You will be amazed at the bargains you can secure. Unless you have access to cash, your only problem will be securing the credit.

### Financing

It is important to shop around for the financing just as you did for the car itself. Dealers sometimes make more profit on the financing than they do on the car itself. Special advertised rates by the manufacturer's financial institutions may be great deals, but it is always worth-while to compare the rates with your bank or other credit institutions.

That said, don't automatically discount garage offers. Many have a large pool of money, enabling them to get good deals on credit.

Most importantly, avoid balloon payments. The deal that offers you cheap monthly repayments may not be so cheap when you realise you have to pay off a huge lump sum at the end of five years. With depreciation and wear-and-tear, your car may not be worth as much as the balance by the end of the loan term and you could end up in negative equity.

But what if you want a car and don't have a large wodge of cash, a desire to be in debt or access to credit?

## Bangernomics

I am a massive fan of bangernomics, which is the art of buying perfectly good old cars at knockdown prices and keeping them running until it's no longer financially viable to do so.

One of the great things about the bangernomics philosophy is that you can afford a far better car than you would be able to choose if you were buying new, or nearly new. It'll also be far cheaper to insure. There are other advantages, not least that you get to show the neighbours that you couldn't care less about keeping up with them.

Indeed, there's a certain shabby chic in driving a 20-year-old BMW estate, as I do. This car, which owes me nothing, has dived so deep into the depreciation trough it'd need to be fitted with a bumper-mounted exploration drill to go any further. So what if it's a bit bashed up? A car never broke down because of a dented door or rusty tailgate.

The fact that – bar driving it into a canal – I can't make it depreciate any more than it has already means I get to bash – without caring – into pillars and supermarket trolleys while parking. Many's the ignorantly parked SUV that has felt my wrath.

You may be concerned that a decade-old car will be unreliable. Not necessarily so. If a car is still on the road after ten years that shows it has been built to last and, if properly maintained, will probably do at least another ten.

That said, when buying a banger it is vital to check the service history. Inspect it thoroughly and if you have any doubts at all or there are suspicious gaps, walk away. Be warned that an NCT only tells you that the car isn't a death trap. It's not a guarantee of mechanical soundness.

Take it from me: if you find yourself a solid, well-built old car from a reputable manufacturer, with a full service history and a lengthy NCT, you'll never look at a new car again.

There is, of course, the argument that older cars have a greater environmental impact than newer ones. It's indisputable that a car built two decades ago will emit far more pollution than one built in 2008. However, very often a car uses more energy and produces more pollution in its manufacture and disposal than in the whole of its working life. So, by keeping an old car on the road instead of scrapping it and buying a brand new one, you may actually be doing more for the environment than someone driving a low-emissions hybrid. That's my argument anyway, and I'm sticking to it.

If you plan to keep a car until it's scrap, you should consider servicing it yourself. As you've no intention of selling it, service history no longer matters. If a garage tells you that servicing your car is a difficult, time-consuming business, they are lying. I can do mine in half an hour and I'm a ham-fisted nincompoop. Why pay some grease monkey €80 an hour to change your sparkplugs and drain your oil when you can buy a Haynes manual for €20 and learn to do it yourself? I'm not suggesting you teach yourself to strip and rebuild the engine, but do learn the basics of keeping your car in good nick. Be aware that prevention is better than cure. If you don't fix a leaky €10 pipe, it could lead to a blown head gasket costing thousands to repair.

Be careful though. Make sure you know exactly what you are doing before you fly headlong under the bonnet. If you make a hames of your engine, it may cost you far more to get it fixed than it would have if you had let a professional do it in the first place. It's probably also good advice to never try to tinker with anything that will kill you if you get it wrong.

While on the subject of older cars, there's always the option of a classic, which is defined under the eyes of the law as any car over 30 years old. If you do very limited mileage and are happy to get your hands dirty under a bonnet, this can be a great option. Road tax for classic cars is a pittance, there is no NCT required and depreciation is not an issue. Indeed, if the car is well-maintained and desirable, you might even make money when you sell it.

Insurance can be an issue, however. Many companies won't touch classics, while others will only insure one if you already have another car insured with them. The way around this is to get it insured under your significant other's policy, assuming they have one, and agree a limited mileage policy. I did that with my 1975 BMW 2002 and it cost me just a couple of hundred euro a year to insure.

Fuel costs may be high, but if you are merely using it to potter around at weekends that's hardly a major consideration. You'll be saving enough in tax already to make it worth it. And you'll have a smile on your face every time you get behind the wheel.

**Insurance**

When was the last time you really looked at your insurance policy? Do you automatically renew it when the year is up, or do you actively seek ways of reducing your outlay? You could be wasting hundreds of euro a year. Ask yourself this: do you really need fully comprehensive insurance? Can you do without some of the bells and whistles your insurer is offering?

If you are with the Automobiles Association (AA), why are you paying an insurance company for breakdown cover? And, conversely, if your insurance company automatically provides breakdown cover free of charge, why are you with the AA? You should consider dropping collision coverage on older cars that aren't worth much. Any claim you make probably won't exceed the cost of the insurance and the deductible amount.

You can also ask for a larger excess, which is the amount of money you have to cough up before your insurance policy comes to the rescue. If, for example, your excess is €500, you could increase it to €1,000. This still covers you against serious damage, but it may decrease your monthly premium by as much as 30 per cent. If you resign yourself to paying for the little dings and dents and leave the really big stuff to the insurance company, you can save a fortune.

When you are shopping around for insurance, haggle. Most drivers are shy about negotiating their premium. If you have, for example, a clean driving licence or expensive car alarm fitted, make a point of it and ask for a discount. If you don't ask, you don't get.

And don't be afraid to bounce one company off the other. Fib if needs be. Tell your insurer that McShyster's down the road has offered you exactly the same cover for €100 less. They may check. But they may not. They might just match or better the other 'offer'. Insurers know that there is precious little brand loyalty in the car insurance industry. If they want your business badly enough, they will find a way to match the competition. Even if you've made it up.

Is this moral? Perhaps not. But this is the insurance industry we're talking about. They make hundreds of millions of euro profit each year.

## Fuel

When it comes to fuel costs, it doesn't take a genius to work out that using less of the stuff can save you a bundle. But how best to do it?

You may think that your car is designed to do 'x' number of kilometres to the litre no matter what you do, but you'd be wrong. Your driving habits can have a massive impact on fuel economy. It's not difficult. Just use your common sense. For a start, have a look inside your car. Hauling around unnecessary weight costs you money. How much junk are you hauling around? Do you have a boot full of golf clubs, paving slabs, turf or power tools? Do you really need all this stuff? Really? When is the last time you used your roof rack? A roof rack can decrease your fuel economy by 10 per cent. Do you need yours or are you just too lazy to take it off? Air conditioning uses loads of fuel. Turn it off. Open windows also cause drag. Close them.

Keep your car serviced and the tyres inflated to the recommended pressure. Underinflated tires can increase rolling resistance by 1.4 per cent for every 1 psi drop in pressure in all four tyres. Don't rely on your sat nav. Use a map too. It may reveal a shorter route. If you are stuck in traffic, turn the engine off. Don't drive around a whole car park looking for the handiest space. Take the first spot you see and walk. Reverse into parking spaces. It's far more efficient to reverse a warm-engined car than a cold one.

On the open road, try to maintain a consistent speed. Fuel economy is maximised when acceleration and braking are minimised. Try to anticipate what's happening ahead. Learn to cruise to a halt, dropping a gear and letting the engine do the work, rather than whacking on the brakes. Don't shoot off from traffic lights like a boy racer on speed. Accelerate slowly and smoothly. Once at cruising speed, drive in a high gear to keep the revs low.

Keep an eye on fuel-pricing websites like www. pumps.ie for fluctuating costs. While it's hardly worth driving 20 kilometres out of your way to save a measly 1 cent per litre, if you see that one station near you is consistently cheaper than others, modify your routine to enable you to drive by it. You can save up to €5 on a tank of fuel by shopping around.

While the above are fairly self-evident measures that any motorist can and should take, they're not enough for some people. There is a growing global movement of motorists taking fuel conservation to an extreme. These pioneers are the proponents of hypermiling, the art of maximising car efficiency. There's another word for it: nenpimania, which translates as an unhealthy obsession with fuel economy. And obsession it is. For hypermilers employ all manner of tricks – some obvious, some cunning, some downright dangerous – to increase their fuel economy.

These include lightening the car's load by extreme measures, such as taking out all the seats except the driver's or removing internal trim and covering the radiator grille with cardboard for aerodynamic reasons. They also shun idling, accelerating wildly, using rough roads, sitting in traffic, headwinds and driving in the rain. The land where they live must be a windless desert full of empty roads paved with fresh tarmac. Some also turn off their engines while cruising down hills and coast up to traffic lights in neutral. Advanced hypermilers have even been known to drive with one set of tires on the white lane markers to reduce rolling resistance. Some hypermilers overinflate their tyres to cut resistance, safety be damned.

While this is not recommended – as it could lead to pulverisation – some even 'draft' behind trucks, thus reducing drag. And their life expectancy.

Of course, the best way to save fuel is to get out and push. Or, better still, ditch the car altogether.


## How to Live without a Car

We Irish love cars. We persistently feature towards the top of the European Union lists for both car ownership and hours spent behind the wheel. There are many reasons for this, including the unfeasibility of relying on public transport for many people.

People love the freedom their car provides them with, not only to get around but to be alone with themselves, cocooned in their comfortable little boxes where they can warble Mariah Carey or engage in some deep nasal mining to their heart's content, untroubled by spouse, kids or other nuisances.

But have you ever asked yourself if you really need your car? Could you get by without it, even for a few days a week? While you may recoil in horror at the thought, it may actually be more doable than you think. You could also save a small fortune. In July 2008, the Dublin Transportation Office said the average car commute in Dublin cost almost €2,000 a year, or €37 a week. In addition, it said Dublin motorists could save €250 a year if they left their cars at home for just one day every week.

There are lots of modern conveniences we're so used to that we think we'd be lost without them. Three years ago, I'd never heard of an MP3 player. Now I think my head would burst if I lost mine. But would it? Of course not. I'd get used to it and find an alternative way to blot out the inane witterings of my fellow humans. A car is no different. It may seem obvious, but if you live in an area with decent public transportation, take advantage of it. What you sacrifice in terms of your own personal space and liberty to veer off course if need be, you'll make up for in savings and convenience.

I'm a big fan of trains myself. They are quick, environmentally friendly and, unlike a bike or car, you can fall asleep on them and still get home alive.

Or how about carpooling? The Internet is riddled with carpooling websites, many of which, like www.carpoolworld.com and www.carshare.com, are open to Irish users, while www.dublintraffic.ie also offers bulletin boards for carpoolers as well as an option to register specific details about commuting routes. In addition, Swift Commute (www.swiftcommute.ie) offers an advanced system that matches potential carpoolers based on their map co-ordinates.

So there's probably a car-pooling website covering your area. If there isn't, why not set one up? You could be a pioneer. If you don't fancy the idea of sharing with a stranger, canvass your neighbours instead. Find one who works within striking distance of you and cadge a lift one day, returning the favour the next. It's a win-win situation.

Should you be within cycling distance of work, you really ought to take advantage of the Government's offer of benefit-in-kind of up to €1,000 to buy a bicycle and all the ancillary equipment. With the tax incentive, you can save up to €410 on your purchase (as of March 2009). Unless you lose the plot completely in the bike shop and fall for some carbon fibre-framed yoke that costs as much as a small hatchback, a grand is more than enough to buy yourself a solid, reliable commuting machine and all the necessary gear.

A good lock is a sound investment. Best of all are D-locks made of hardened steel. While these can be prised open with car-jacks, you'd have to be very unlucky to be targeted by such dedicated thieves. They are, however, extremely heavy and inflexible, making them a pain to carry around and difficult to wrap around some of the odd-shaped objects cyclists are forced to lock their bikes to. A decent compromise is a steel chain with padlock that will deter all but the most determined thieves.

Sadly, the truth is no lock is invincible. If a crook has the tools and wants your bike, there's not a lot you can do about it other than gaffer-taping it to your leg. Speaking of which, pay attention to what you lock your bike to. I once had an expensive mountain bike locked with three chains to a bar that was bolted into a concrete wall in an underground garage. When I came downstairs in the morning, thieves had wangled their way through the electric gates and unbolted the bar from the wall, taking the bike, locks and all. I was more than a tad peeved. But also a little bit impressed.

Once you have a bike and gear, cycling is free. Not only that, but it's environmentally friendly, you can park where you like, you don't have to pay tax or insurance and you're immune to traffic congestion. It's great for giving yourself a cardiovascular workout and – assuming you don't get splatted by some egomaniac in an SUV – it is a no-impact sport.

Alternatively, buy a moped, scooter or small motor-cycle. They are relatively inexpensive to buy, insure, maintain and operate, and are fun to ride. Especially through traffic, when you can grin smugly at the motorists foundering in car porridge as you zip along.

Many potential cyclists are put off by the rain factor. They needn't be. Contrary to popular perception, it's not that wet in Ireland. According to Met Éireann, the average number of 'wet' days ranges from about 150 days a year along the east and south-east coasts, to about 225 days a year in parts of the west. However, a day is deemed 'wet' if a mere 1 mm of rain falls over the course of 24 hours. This is nothing. You'd get wetter being licked by a Labrador than cycling or motorcycling to work on a 1 mm day. It only really, really pours on around 20 days a year. Honest.

For many people, it'd simply be unrealistic to get rid of their cars altogether. But by taking a few small steps to cut down on unnecessary trips and using alternative transport where possible instead, you can take a huge weight off your wallet.

It may take some adjustment, but it'll be worth it in the end.

# 8

# Cut-Price Culture

**Edel Coffey**

In times of recession it's the luxuries that go first. But what constitutes a luxury depends on who you are. One person's necessity can easily be another person's extravagance. For this reason a kind of fuzzy logic reigns in recession, the kind of logic that will see a woman spend her last penny, or should I say last €150, on half-head easi-mesh highlights (necessity item), but flinch at spending one-sixth of that on the unjustifiable expense of a theatre ticket (luxury item).

But there is no need to forego your favourite luxury item or necessities just because money is tight. You can still have that blow-dry and a night out on the town. It's just that now you might need to take the bus into town instead of a taxi and the blow-dry might have to come from the local salon instead of the big-bucks hairdressers in the city centre.

Hairdressers and pubs will probably survive the slump just fine, but some of the biggest victims of the squeeze are what we consider non-essentials, which all too often fall into the 'culture' bracket. We tend to think of art, music, theatre and books as expensive, which can be the case. But there is a wealth of cheap, if not free, ways to experience all of the above too.

When you've got the big trump cards of mortgage payments, food bills, heating expenses and keeping the children clothed and fed vying for your finances, what's left over for culture? Not a lot. But it turns out you don't need a lot of money to have fun. Just a bit of inventiveness.

We may consider culture a non-essential item, but it is what feeds the soul and, in times like these, that is more essential than ever.

### Number Crunch

The Arts Council was awarded a budget of **€76 million** in 2009, down 10 per cent from **€85 million** in 2008, prompting Deputy Chairman Maurice Foley to comment that 'in these difficult times, the enrichment of our lives by the arts is more necessary than ever.' Out of the **352 arts organisations** that were awarded grants in 2009, **68 per cent** saw their funding cut. However, cinemagoers often glue themselves to the silver screen during recessions: box office sales in the UK and Ireland reached a record high of **£950 million** in 2008.

**Nights on the Town**

The vintners would have you believe that the pub is the be-all and end-all of Irish culture, the centre of Irish life and a cosy home-from-home that you'd be happy never to leave. The pub can be all of these things, but just as often it can be dirty and draughty, with staff recruited from Grumpy Men-R-Us. And let's not even get started on the price of the drink. That's something that you're not going to easily get around this recession-tide.

God be with the days when there was such a thing as 'Happy Hour'. The word 'hour' was loosely interpreted and in some places it lasted up to four hours. As that kind of fun is now strictly verboten, the easiest way to have a cheaper night in the pub is to start a little later in the public house and a little earlier in the private house. That is, have some friends around to share a bottle of wine and some nibbles, then arrive at the pub at nine o'clock instead of seven feeling convivial and aglow. Instant money-saver.

Avoid rounds at all costs. They will make you bankrupt and more drunk than you need to be. They are a vulgar and inappropriate display of wealth in a time of recession, and nobody should be expected to get involved in them. Try interspersing each drink with a glass of sparkling or (gasp) tap water. Okay, so it sounds a bit ascetic but it will dilute the cost of a night out, not to mention your hangover the next day. If you can't stand to do this, try drinking a spritzer or shandy between 'proper' drinks.

Beware of bars where prices go up as the evening wears on. Some bars charge more for a drink after 11 o'clock than before, so something as simple as getting your order in at five-to instead of five-past can make all the difference.

There is one other tried and tested way to save money in bars and still manage to drink as much as you like. Novel idea: allow the man or woman of your fancy to buy you a drink.

## Slump-Time Screen-Time

Cinema offers a good, cheap alternative to a night out, although how much cheaper depends on where in the country you're living. Dubliners pay almost 10 per cent more for cinema tickets than those outside the capital. In Dublin, the average cinema ticket on a Saturday night will cost €10 per adult. It's the add-ons like popcorn, drinks and nibbles that bring the combined bill for two people closer to €40.

It sounds mean but, if you buy a drink and snacks in the newsagent's on the corner before going to the cinema, this will drastically reduce your overheads. (Don't do this if you're on a date though, as you will look stingy.)

There are ways to cut the price of tickets too, however. Some of the bigger Cineplexes offer unlimited monthly or annual tickets, which easily pay for themselves if you attend the cinema twice a month. Taking in a movie on a weeknight or during the day will slash the price of your ticket (and this is often more enjoyable, as the cinema is emptier and quieter).

If you're not a cinemagoer, renting DVDs is a cheaper option still, with new releases costing on average €5.50 (although in some cinemas you may be able to get to watch a big-screen flick for not much more than that on a weekday, if you avoid the popcorn counter). DVD rental stores offer great value on television series box sets, which cost an average of €10 for seven nights.

In straitened times, television will be where people see most of their celluloid delights, although it is an expensive proposition in these high definition pay-per-view times. If you are buying anything more advanced than the basic cable package, you can pay up to €70 a month. Take a cold, hard look at the basic cable package, compare it to your current digital package and ask yourself how many of the supplementary channels you actually watch and how often. A quick and easy way to save money is to downgrade to a basic cable package, which will still offer plenty of variety of channels to satisfy your television needs. It's remarkable how quickly you'll discover that you don't actually miss those four re-runs a day of *Frasier*. And anyway, 25 channels should be enough for anyone.

## MySpace to Mixtapes

There has never been a better time than now to get free music, and I'm not talking illegally either. The idea of paying for music was already becoming archaic before the recession hit and, now that the recession is here, it is positively criminal. Even bands have come round to this way of thinking, with Radiohead and Nine Inch Nails being just two of the international acts who offered radical approaches to selling their music in 2008 (Nine Inch Nails' record was free, while Radiohead's had an administration fee of 49p).

Most bands now offer the option of at least one free download from their official website, MySpace or Last.fm. Last.fm is a great place to listen to free music, as it offers full sample tracks from most artists and usually downloads too. It also gives the option of building a library, so you can store all the songs you love on your user account. MySpace is still one of the original and best places to hear a selection of a band or artist's music, with more and more bands allowing free downloads here too. Of course, you have to pay for broadband to avail of all this music online, but you don't have to sign a contract and pay a monthly bill anymore. Mobile telecoms provider '3' Ireland offers pay-as-you-go broadband (from €19.99 for a month's usage, as of February 2009) and a once-off payment of €39 for the USB modem, which means you can use it anywhere. And there's always the local Internet café.

There are other ways to get free music. Revive the lost art of making a mixtape and ask someone to make a mix-CD for you. Don't forget to make one for them in return.

When it comes to live music, chances are you will have to pay at least a nominal fee to see the music of your choice. Otherwise, you're stuck with the pub covers guy or open mics. Both bad.

But there are plenty of superb live performers who will charge €10 or under on the door and often you'll get a free CD with the entry fee. Some excellent and consistently reliable small promoters are Magical Girl, The Ballroom of Romance and Skinny Wolves, all bringing international and interesting acts to Ireland that you're not likely to get the opportunity to see again, or in such small venues. For listings try www.thumped.com or www.entertainment.ie. If you like live music but don't like crowds, you can always check out www.liveinyourlivingroom.com and www.balcony tv.com for some live music in the comfort of your own home.

**When You've Just Got to Laugh**

Comedy tends to be one of those industries that seems to be recession-proof. Okay, so maybe the big guys won't sell as many nights in Vicar Street, but there is simply no stopping the weekly €5-entry stand-up nights, which will be stuffed with people who believe laughter is the best remedy for these times.

The bi-weekly Mish Mash in the International Bar in Dublin, the pub that is famous as the place where all the big names started, costs just €7. The Laughter Lounges in both Dublin and Belfast run regular comedy nights, while the Neptune Comedy Club on Abbey Street, Dublin runs every Friday night with an entry charge of just €8.

One of the rowdiest places to catch some stand-up is the Ha'Penny Bridge Inn in Dublin (or it has been the nights I've been there), which sees old and new, amateur and pro line up together. Be warned though: if you're no good, you'll know all about it – not a kind crowd.

**Wrapped Up in Books**

Books are one of the most enjoyable of life's free pleasures. Every one of us has access to an endless supply of free (and up-to-date) books from our local library. Libraries are not how you might remember them if you haven't visited one since childhood. They now have wonderful online catalogues so you can search for the book you want before you leave your house. Through your local library you will find details of local book events, including book clubs and reader nights. Click on www.library.ie to find your local library. There's also the new European-wide website www.europeana.eu.

A great way to get rid of your old books and get new ones in their place is www.bookswap.ie and www. bookhopper.ie. Simply become a member of the website and start trading books with other members.

Joining a book club is a great way to meet other readers who will be interested in swapping books and it provides a cheap social occasion, as book clubs are often held in members' own homes with food and drink provided. Second-hand bookshops and most charity shops have a wide selection of current books for a fraction of the original price. There are also huge savings to be had on Amazon's second-hand option (www.amazon.co.uk), while www. AbeBooks.com is one of the Web's best resources for second-hand and rare books.

## Recession Cuisine

Recession is a scary word for everyone, but for restaurants it has the same effect as an infestation of cockroaches – people tend to stay away. A trip to the pub with friends is maintained as one of life's necessities, but a trip to a restaurant, which can cost the same (or even less), is viewed as an outlandish expense. On the other hand, a recession can be good for the customer, bringing out value in restaurants. Mid-priced places like Café Bar Deli, Gourmet Burger and Jo'Burger thrive, offering decent food for a good price with no frills. These are the untouchables in this market, but you can still visit more upmarket restaurants. Those restaurants that have been established for more than a decade often offer remarkable promotions at excellent value. Eating at a restaurant you might have considered out of your budget suddenly becomes possible.

Early bird and pre-theatre specials are the cheapest options, but it does mean you're done and dusted by the time you would normally only be thinking of heading out. Set menus offer another low-cost alternative, giving you a three- or four-course meal for between €20 and €40.

Some restaurants offer excellent promotions on quiet nights so do investigate what your local has on offer (Les Frères Jacques on Dublin's Dame Street does a Monday and Tuesday night special where all its wines are half-price). L'Gueuleton is a recent addition to the Irish restaurant scene and offers great French food for reasonable prices in a charming bistro atmosphere. If you're on a budget, Jade Chinese Restaurant off Capel Street and Gruel on Dame Street both offer hearty, cheap meals. The table set-up in Gruel means you're likely to hear everything the couple sitting next to you have to say to each other, but when the food clocks in at an average of €12 each it's hard to complain. If you want fine dining at home, try Butler's Pantry.

**Trips to the Theatre**

For some reason, theatre in Ireland has a reputation for being a pastime of the rich and aged, despite the fact that it costs on average the same to see a band in a mid-sized venue as it does to see a play in our national theatre. And that's at full price.

It is easy to get to see theatre cheaply. The Abbey offers concession tickets from Monday to Friday and preview and matinée tickets are available at a cheaper price too. Some theatres even offer discounts on group bookings, which is a good excuse to get a group of friends together for a trip to the theatre.

If you think theatre is not for you, perhaps starting with the less traditional theatre groups rather than the more traditional production companies might be a better way into it. Small threatre companies often provide some of the most cutting-edge and entertaining theatre for a fraction of the price. Try Project, Red Kettle or Pan Pan (who did an astonishing modern-day production of *The Playboy of the Western World* in Mandarin).

Save money by opting for the cheapest seats. None of the theatres in Ireland are so big that it will make a difference to your enjoyment of the performance.

Festivals run all year round, with the Dublin Theatre Festival and the Docklands festival We Are Here providing international and groundbreaking theatre year on year. The Dublin Theatre Festival is usually held in September–October and, in recent years, theatergoers have been offered the opportunity to become 'friends' of the festival for a cost-effective price that will give you access to complimentary tickets, premium seats, guest talks and discounted theatre outings throughout the year.

## Art Attack

Art can be as cheap as you want it to be. The museums of this country are places that we tend to take for granted, but they are stuffed to the gills with amazing works of art and are a lovely calming way to pass a few hours amidst the bustle of the city. Ireland has some wonderful museums and galleries with great permanent collections and even better touring ones (there's nearly always a charge for these but, like everywhere, cost often varies depending on when you choose to visit). The National Gallery is a joy to walk around, as is the Irish Museum of Modern Art (IMMA) and, now that it's on the Luas line, you have a way of getting back into town. Give the cafés and shops a miss though as it's here you'll really spend your money. Still, it's always nice to pick up a postcard by your favourite artist, and that's not going to break anybody's bank.

When it comes to buying art, it's a different matter. Buying art is considered a frivolity, but the price of art is defined by the market. Even Damien Hirst had to let some staff go in 2008. Buying art is hardly ever cheap, but in a more stringent market your chances of getting art for less improve as there is less competition.

While you're not likely to get much for under €1,000, most galleries do offer options of paying for a work over a period of time so you don't have to shell out the full amount all at once. If that's out of your budget, numbered prints, sketches or pen-and-ink drawings are wonderful compromises that you can get for much cheaper.

The intimidating world of auction houses is one worth investigating. Auctions can be poorly attended, meaning you can pick up some real bargains and, increasingly, some artists are even bypassing galleries and selling their art directly at auctions.

If you're too intimidated by this idea, start with the markets (Merrion Square is a good one) where you can walk around unmolested. Just don't forget to haggle. You can also buy online, but art is such a subjective thing that it is always best to view a piece in person or at least be familiar with the artist before buying online. Lots of restaurants act as galleries too, while another good place to pick up cheaper works of art is at end-of-year student exhibitions. Well, you never know your luck.

# 9

# Budget Travel: Escaping the Doom and Gloom

## Gareth Naughton

Don't you just feel the urge to run? Economic meltdown and credit crunch be damned. A few months on the other side of the world where you can't read the newspapers and the television shows wall-to-wall Japanese game shows sounds like heaven right now. And, indeed, it may just be the perfect time to go travelling – inevitably, as the financial screws tighten, fewer people are taking the plunge, so those who can are going to be treated extremely well by worried airlines, hoteliers and restaurateurs.

Still, make no mistake, taking a year out is an expensive business. The cost of your trip will depend greatly on your destinations, but you should be budgeting for around €1,000 per month outside of flight costs. That probably sounds like a lot, but you will be paying for nightly accommodation, all food and drink, transport, activities, visas and bribes for local officials – not to mention the woeful amount of money you will lose thanks to the many rip-off artists you will encounter on your way. If a man in a turban approaches you and starts babbling on about your lucky number, tell him to hump off immediately and if your taxi driver offers to take you on a 'tour' for a suspiciously cheap price, make a dash for it. In any case, it all mounts up.

## Number Crunch

Faced with shrinking numbers of foreign visitors, the Irish tourist industry will be hoping that cash-strapped holiday-makers opt for 'staycations' (stay-at-home vacations) during the slump. But in the first nine months of 2008, spending by Irish residents on domestic trips was down **2 per cent** compared to a year earlier, with fewer people taking longer holidays. Meanwhile, spending on international travel rose **6 per cent**, as people continued to make room in their budgets for overseas trips.

### Location, Location, Location

Just like property, travel is all about location, location, location, and, if you want to save money, it's about picking the road less travelled. If you follow the crowd, you will inevitably end up in tourist or backpacker traps where everything is just that little bit more expensive than elsewhere. This applies across the board – not just to backpackers. A city break in Paris is clearly going to be more expensive than a few nights in Tallinn, and two weeks in the Costa del Sol (cheap apartment and all) is going to set you back more than a fortnight on the Black Sea. Don't blame the locals – it's not their fault that the average Irish traveller boasts the sense of adventure of a librarian. Of course they are going to take advantage.

You can avoid the frustration of feeling ripped off by visiting places less popular with your fellow Westerners. That does not mean that you should aim to take up residence with an undiscovered tribe in the Borneo jungle.

It does mean looking for accommodation that's just a little bit out of the way and being smart about it. Secluded places might be heavenly to look at but they can be boring after a while, particularly if it is difficult to get to the nearest bit of life. Still, with transportation so cheap – after a couple of months travelling in South-East Asia you'll be walking around Dublin feeling offended that no-one has offered you a lift – staying a couple of beaches away from the main action shouldn't be a problem.

I stayed in a very basic €2-per-night Thai beach hut once. Unfortunately, it cost another €5 to get to the nearest town and it was difficult to get back after a night on the tiles. Small change it may be but these things add up. Two beaches over is fine but the other side of the island? Foolhardy. Still, wobbling slightly off the beaten track will save you money and also give you the more authentic experience that the self-righteous bores who write travel books insist you must have (though they often seem to think this rests on visiting Chinatown everywhere you land, which is equivalent to telling someone Temple Bar is authentic Ireland).

Being realistic about how much you are going to need will make for a more comfortable journey. So you found a beach hut on a beautiful and relatively deserted stretch of sand in the Gulf of Thailand for €2 a night? Fair play to you, but that's just a place to rest your head. You will still be spending money. You'll need to eat, drink, pay locals a pittance to ferry you back and forth, and of course money to cross the palm of the local guru who promises to bring you spiritual enlightenment. And, much as you would like to, staying there forever is not a possibility. Granted, you may not spend that much in a month, but better to be over-resourced than have to spend a month eating cheese and bread stolen from your youth hostel because you're short of cash.

If you are travelling on a limited budget and want your money to stretch a long way, you should probably eliminate North America, Australia and New Zealand from your itinerary. Accommodation costs in North America will drain your bank account faster than you can say 'have a nice day', and travelling in such a vast country is both difficult and expensive. Similarly, Australia and New Zealand have lots to offer someone who is looking for the trip of a lifetime, but you are going to pay for it. Ditto for Japan and Western Europe. Throw an extra €500 on your monthly budget if your heart is set on Sydney, San Francisco or Tokyo.

The hottest travel destination for backpackers at the moment is South America, and the good news is that your money goes a very long way once you are there. However, flights to Latin America can be expensive. Flights to South-East Asia, however, are ten a penny and tend to be cheaper, and here, too, your money stretches phenomenally. That said, South-East Asia is swarming with backpackers (particularly of the grating 18-year-old gap-year kind), so, if you are looking for uncharted territory, look elsewhere.

Sticking to the long established backpacker trail can be both a blessing and a curse. The road well travelled is there for a reason. However, it is very easy to find yourself bussing it from one backpacker ghetto to another. Even though it may seem relatively cheap, it's far more likely that you are getting ripped off.

Every guidebook for Bangkok, for instance, will steer you in the direction of the Khao San Road with its abundance of guesthouses and plethora of bars selling cheap beer and toasted cheese sandwiches. Try taking a taxi anywhere from there and you'll find that a journey that should cost €1 ends up costing €3 because your friendly Thai taxi man won't turn on the meter. That's the tip of the iceberg. Getting away from the ghettos – even just around the corner – will have you pleasantly surprised by how much cheaper everything is.

You can significantly reduce your outlay before you leave by cajoling one of your friends to join you. Sharing costs on accommodation and food will obviously save you cash in the long run, and having a friend to travel with will ensure that you don't resort to talking to your friendly beach hut cockroaches for company. Plus, should you get kidnapped, there's someone there to raise the alarm. Always comforting.

Fear not if you are planning on flying solo, however. While it is a daunting prospect, once you start travelling you'll find heaps of people in a similar situation. Milk them for all they're worth – listen to their advice when it comes to cheap, decent places to stay and the best places to visit. A bit of brazenness goes a long way and these new friends can be your ticket to a cheaper trip. Hooking up with a like-minded someone and agreeing to share accommodation, food, taxis and so on should also be considered.

One of the best ways to reduce costs in Australia or the USA when there's more than one of you is to hire a campervan. It acts as both your accommodation for the night and transport, and gives you real freedom to do what you choose. For the more rugged amongst us, hiring (or even buying) a car and setting up camp wherever you land will do the same job. Bear in mind you will have to pay for petrol and, in some cases, a berth for the night at a caravan park or camping ground. If you are travelling alone, you can still do this – advertise at your youth hostel or an Internet café for someone heading in the same direction who would be willing to share costs and driving. Make sure they are hygienically sound before committing to anything – campervans are small, very small.

Tread carefully if joining forces with a new companion. After all, strangers can be, well, strange. On a recent trip

101

to Bali, a friend and I were lumbered with a tremendously boring stranger who we accidentally acquired at the airport and whom we couldn't shake for ten days. By day five it was all getting a bit *Lord of the Flies*. If that happens to you, make a midnight run or just storm off in the middle of the day as we did. It's not like you are ever going to see them again.

You can also reduce costs by choosing to take long-distance buses, trains and ferries. These can be unbelievably cheap compared to flying but you are sacrificing serious amounts of time and, sometimes, comfort by taking this cheaper option. After seven-and-a-half hours sitting on top of a very rocky boat from Bali to the Gili islands with two iron bars between us and the very deep blue sea, I opted for the fast boat back. Twice the price, one-third the travel time, 100 per cent less likely to end in death. A no-brainer. In general, if you are willing to lose a bit of time and take a bit of discomfort, bus, train or ferry are good options. You will also get to gloat about how terribly environmentally friendly it all was. Just make sure that whatever mode of transport you choose is safe – consult with other travellers in person or online – before you commit.

### Flying Without Things

Being clever when booking your flights can also save you serious cash. Some of this is obvious stuff but it bears saying. The earlier you book, the more likely you are to score a good deal and do not procrastinate if you spot one. Flight costs change on a daily basis and, as the date approaches, will skyrocket. Being flexible with your dates and, indeed, aiming to fly mid-week, late at night or early in the morning should bring the price down significantly. If you find a good deal on websites like www.ebookers.ie or www.gohop.ie, cross-check it with the relevant airline's own website – sometimes they can offer you a better deal.

The most obvious option is to buy a round-the-world ticket. These come in a variety of options and cover a good portion of the planet. Well, the bits worth visiting anyway. It is important to note, however, that most round-the-world tickets only give you a year to complete the circuit. It is their biggest drawback and if you are planning on spending a year working in Australia, New Zealand, the US or Canada, a round-the-world ticket will probably be too restrictive for you. Consider booking an open-ended return flight and make the most of the free stopovers available.

Since Michael O'Leary started his one-man crusade to make air travel as cheap and as stressful as possible, no-frills flying is a worldwide epidemic. This is particularly true in South-East Asia where Air Asia and Tiger Airways have established extensive networks (including long distance flights to Oz) at almost-Ryanair prices. Of course, with fuel prices bouncing all over the place, airlines are currently demonstrating all the stability of a Big Brother housemate, so pay by credit card to give you some security.

If you are going to go down the no-frills route, it will pay to keep a tight rein on the weight of your backpack. Inevitably, you won't need half the stuff you are carrying around. Giant bottles of shampoo and rakes of charming yet useless tat bought from super-friendly beach sellers are unnecessary. With Air Asia, you pay a small fee to check in a bag weighing up to 15 kilos. Anything over that – even if you pay to book in two or three bags – will incur excess baggage charges. It's a good idea to keep your backpack light anyway. As someone who lugged 22 kilos around South-East Asia (forcing my infuriated travelling companion to pack and repack bags at various Air Asia desks), I can't tell you how often I felt like dumping the damn thing in the nearest murky brown river and starting over. Indeed, I started bartering my stuff for lighter things. It's amazing what you can get for a tatty five-year-old shirt.

You can also keep costs down by combining flights with a no-frills airline to, for instance, an Asian hub like Bangkok with a flight with one of the standard carriers to London and then a cheap Ryanair, Aer Lingus or bmibaby flight back to Dublin. There is a lot of hassle involved in collecting bags and checking them in again, so weigh that up against the savings made. Starting your journey proper in London should also be considered – with a far greater number of airlines to choose from, competition is intense and it is possible to save hundreds by organising your own first leg from Dublin to London.

## Youth Host-Hell

In many countries, your cheapest accommodation option, short of sleeping under the stars, will be a youth hostel. With a constant inflow of backpackers, both Australia and New Zealand are teeming with youth hostels – you will find them in even the smallest towns on the backpacker trail and in some places they may be your only option. In America, youth hostels are largely confined to the cities. Venture into Deliverance country, however, and grotty motels are your cheapest option.

Youth hostels are an acquired taste. On the plus side, they offer a cheap bed for the night, special offers that will bring down your food and drink costs, and access to like-minded travellers. However, there's a reason they are called youth hostels. If you are over 25 and fancy a good night's sleep at some point during your travels, *youth* hostels are not your friend.

Staying at a youth hostel requires great patience, an ability to sleep in small and uncomfortable beds, a good set of ear plugs and a healthy attitude to the semi-naked (or often naked) body in all its grotesque forms. Make no mistake about it, your fellow hostel dwellers are dirty buggers. If listening to other people attempt to fiddle with each other quietly in a room full of strangers is your thing, you've found heaven. I once had the grave misfortune of staying in a youth hostel in Hawaii – I know, poor me – where the man in the bunk across from me spent an entire night alternating between having sex and smoking crack with a member of the world's oldest profession. But he put a blanket up so that was okay. We were a bit green around the gills so we didn't complain. In retrospect, we should have had him thrown out. Nobody wants to be a prude, but if you wanted a sex show you would nip down to the local red light district.

A couple of things make youth hostel stays easier. Even though it might cost a couple of euro more, it is well worth upgrading to a dorm with fewer beds. Landing yourself in a room with 7 to 23 strangers is a recipe for mass-murder-inducing frustration. Most youth hostels will have a variety of accommodation options on offer – if on your own, go for the one that offers the most privacy. If you are travelling in a couple or are so tight with your travelling companion that spooning is par for the course, a private room at a hostel offers the best of both worlds. Basic private rooms with a double bed generally cost a little more than two dorm beds and you can still enjoy the benefits of being in a youth hostel.

Do a bit of research before you decide to book. Websites like www.hostelbookers.com and www.hostelworld.com feature user-generated ratings that are usually fairly accurate. Talk to travellers who have visited before or ask for advice on a traveller's forum like www.lonelyplanet.com/thorntree and you should get a steer in the right direction. And, seriously, invest in a really good set of ear plugs. If you can wear an eye mask without looking like Elizabeth Taylor or Julian Clary, do it.

Happily, if you stick to South-East Asia and South America, you may never need to set foot inside a youth hostel because guesthouse and hotel accommodation – ranging from the very basic to the opulent – remain relatively cheap. With such an abundance of accommodation available, it is not always necessary to book in advance – although you should check out when the local festivals are to ensure you don't arrive just as the place starts to heave, pushing you out on the street. But, in general, there is no need for advance booking, unless your crunch-proof budget means you can afford to stay somewhere terribly swanky. Ask to see the room before you commit and stay one night before committing to a longer stay. Do not be afraid to argue over the price. The savings might seem pointless, but a bit of haggling is expected and you'll save the cost of a night's drinking over a couple of weeks.

Enough cash to stretch to the odd hotel or two? Don't waste it. Use a forum like www.tripadvisor.com for tips on good-value hotels at your destination of choice. Tripadvisor also has a user-generated review system and ranks hotels accordingly. When reading the reviews, you should bear in mind that one man's five-star hotel is another man's one-star flea pit (American and Singaporean contributors, in particular, seem to have impossibly high expectations).

Excellent discounts are to be found on websites like www.expedia.com, www.lastminute.com and www.wotif. com. The Web is littered with good offers. The latter two sites offer a secret hotels section where you book rooms at massive discounts knowing just the location and the hotel's facilities. It's certainly worth taking a punt. Look carefully at the other hotels listed and you'll be able to identify the 'secret' hotel from its facilities and score a real bargain.

Chance your arm and ask for an upgrade when you arrive (couples should try ringing ahead and claiming they are on honeymoon). Granted you may look and feel a bit of a tight-arse but there's no harm in trying. In these harsh economic times, hoteliers are going to be feeling the pinch more than most. They should be delighted to get your custom. Make them work for your money.

Indeed, no matter where you go, don't be afraid to haggle. In most countries, a bit of bargaining is expected. Don't take it to extremes, however. You know you've been travelling too long when you start fighting with people over the equivalent of 70 cent. That said, you are not a bank (though you probably have more money than some banks at the moment) so don't allow yourself to be steamrolled into paying above the odds. Even in Western countries where haggling is not commonplace, there's no harm asking for the best price possible, especially if it is something expensive.

Finally, don't forget that – unforeseen romantic entanglements with hot (or just visa-hot) Australians or Americans aside – you will be coming home at some point. Tedious as it may sound, the blow of being back in Ireland with the pressures of getting a job, finding a place to live and reacquainting yourself with your friends and family (if they remember that you exist) will be softened if you prepare in advance. Set aside a reasonable sum of money that will act as start-up money on your return and be strong-willed enough not to access it during your travels. Unless the economy makes a stunning return to full employment, you are probably going to be joining the dole queue when you get back. And if you can live off that, you'll be a miracle worker.

WHEN TIMES GET TOUGH

# 10

# Life After Redundancy

## Tom McGuinness

Being made redundant has a different effect on everyone. For a fortunate few, it is welcomed as a means of collecting a pot of money and moving on to pastures new. For most, however, it is a traumatic, unsettling experience and, as with all experiences of this nature, people are generally bewildered as to why it is happening to them.

### Number Crunch

More than **6,700** people were made redundant in January 2009 – the highest ever number of people to become eligible for the Department of Enterprise, Trade and Employment's Redundancy Payments Scheme in a single month. The number of redundancies was **143 per cent** higher than in January 2008, as employers across all sectors of the economy found they were no longer doing enough trade to afford to retain their staff.

Along with these feelings, applying for benefits and dealing with the associated bureaucracy may cause you anxiety. This is natural but will soon change as you begin to move on.

Remember, redundancy is not personal, even though it can feel like it is. The causes are invariably outside your control. Feeling sorry for yourself, and indeed your colleagues, is natural. However, the sooner you turn this negative energy into positive action the better. Even in these turbulent times, when talk of recession is commonplace, opportunities exist to move on, and there are ways to recover and establish yourself on a new and even more exciting career track.

### Moving On: Goal Setting

It is important to redirect your focus as soon as possible from your current uncertain situation to the more positive aspects of the future. Setting a personal goal is an excellent way of focusing your efforts and emotions as you embark on carving out a new and prosperous future for yourself. Initially, this goal should be practical and short term. It could be related to doing up a CV, assessing your financial position or clarifying your entitlements.

The rules of good goal setting are simple:

- State your goal in clear terms – be specific.
- Visualise what is involved and what it will be like to achieve it.
- List the steps to achieving it.
- Break down larger goals into smaller ones if possible.
- Set out your goals in a systematic way.
- Make sure your first goal is achievable as this will build confidence.

You may be driven by a high degree of anxiety at this stage. So, if possible, get someone you know and trust to guide and support you at this stage. Some companies provide career transition support to help you move on and find a new job. Make sure to avail of this help.

As you grow in confidence and your situation becomes clearer, you will be in a better position to consider the bigger picture and set goals for your future career direction. Perhaps this is an opportunity to explore an area you have always been interested in. Maybe you felt somewhat dissatisfied with your job even before you were made redundant. Fear of change may have prevented you from seeking out new opportunities. Being pushed off the deep end makes for a completely new scenario where there are new and exciting opportunities.

Think about turning redundancy into an opportunity to explore the many possibilities that are available today. For example, further education could lead to new career paths. A job in a different sector may provide more security and even better benefits. Becoming your own boss may fulfill a long-cherished dream. Working from home may provide a more family-friendly lifestyle. List out the possibilities and consider them before dismissing any of them too quickly.

There are many examples of people who, following redundancy, started their own businesses and are now running thriving companies. One individual turned his love of gardening into a successful landscape business; another turned her interest in fashion into a dressmaking enterprise. Many of these people will say that redundancy was one of the best things that ever happened to them, though perhaps it did not seem so when they first heard about it. Others have returned to further education or training that was not available to them in early life.

As a first step, get onto the Internet. The Internet has many sources of information ranging from how to prepare a winning CV, to ways of seeking out the right education and career opportunities, to exploring job and business opportunities. Also, most companies have websites that provide practical and useful information, enabling you to be well prepared for interviews or even to customise your CV to better suit the prospective employer's requirements. However, before you take off in a new direction, it is well worth assessing your situation carefully and what you have to offer.

## Assessing Your Situation

A major part of assessing your own situation is to identify as clearly and objectively as possible the skills you have developed over the years. These fall into three categories:

### 1. Personal skills

This is a wide category of skills encompassing your attitude and behaviour. These skills can affect everything from the way you communicate with others to the way you organise your professional life. Qualities such as enthusiasm, the ability to listen and good humour are of increasing appeal to employers. Personal skills enable you to deploy all the other technical and vocational skills that are referred to below.

### 2. Job-specific skills

These are the skills that you have acquired at work or in education and may include craft skills, machine operation, driving and so on. The ability to understand and operate quality control systems, undertake stock checks, manage documentation and compile reports are just a few of the skills that can be considered under this heading. If you had a job specification in your former employment, it may help you to list these skills.

### 3. Transferable skills

Transferable skills are those we possess that are useful across a large number of disciplines, if not all vocations. For example, IT skills are beneficial in a wide range of jobs, as are leadership and linguistic skills. Project management, presentation, analytical and problem-solving skills are other examples of transferable skills.

You may have experience of coaching and mentoring, some of which you may have derived from your recreational pursuits. Do not forget these when making your assessment. Skills associated with working in a team environment and achieving results are increasingly sought after by employers in today's work environment.

## Seeking Out Opportunities

Having reflected on your personal situation, it's time to consider in what way you wish to progress your career. Deciding on your preferred choices will enable you to keep your job search focused.

Any action that aids your search for a new job is valuable and a good CV is crucial to your success. Spending time preparing your CV is time well spent. Do not be afraid to get assistance with its preparation. Whether or not you are called for interview by a prospective employer will depend on your CV. Keep it simple. Ensure that what is included is accurate and clear. Your CV should be:

- Neatly typed.
- Carefully laid out.
- In black and white.
- Not more than three sheets of A4 quality paper.
- Accompanied by a cover letter.

Here are some general tips to make your CV stand out:

- Be positive in your language and presentation.
- Highlight your achievements with specific short examples.
- Make sure that the achievements relate as far as possible to the key requirements, where they are known, of the new job.

On the other hand, there are things to avoid when creating a CV:

- Use of jargon or pretentious language.
- Telling untruths about your skills or achievements.
- Inventing information.
- Copying someone else's CV.
- Rambling on about a particular aspect.

When preparing a CV with a particular employer in mind, start by finding out what the employer is looking for and tailor your CV to this as much as possible. Many companies, particularly if they are using recruitment agencies, will send out standard forms, on request, for you to fill in.

Having prepared the best possible CV, you have to decide where to send it. The first targets will be FÁS and the recruitment agencies. You will have registered with FÁS anyway if you are claiming social welfare entitlements. Try to select recruitment agencies that specialise in your field, as these will understand you and will be better aware of what opportunities are available.

The second range of possibilities will be positions advertised in the media and on websites. Do not forget to look up past editions of newspapers as well as the current ones.

The third focus will be on companies in the region or locality who may be recruiting candidates but who may not have advertised. Most people agree that the best jobs are never advertised but are filled by word of mouth.

Each of us has built up networks over the years, either through work or recreation, and this can be a fourth option open to us. Simply put, networks are people we know who have a range of contacts with other people, some of whom might be useful in this situation. Contacting individuals in your networks who may be aware of companies with vacancies within their extended networks is a very powerful and often undervalued way of seeking out job opportunities. Many people feel shy about doing this, but it is worthwhile overcoming this reserve as the dividends can be high.

Remember that you will not receive responses from many of the companies to which you have sent your CV. This may not be a reflection on you, but on them. They may be too busy or they may not have the systems in place to respond. Be patient and resilient. This is probably the most frustrating part of the job search process but, with persistence, success will be achieved.

Is it worth taking a less-than-perfect position on a full-time basis as an interim solution? This obviously depends on your circumstances. Leaving aside social welfare and income considerations, this may be a beneficial interim solution, provided it does not significantly interfere with your job search. Having somewhere to go every day and remaining in useful employment helps restore confidence and encourages a sense of well-being. The additional experience may also prove useful.

**Being a Successful Interviewee**

Needless to say, arriving on time for the interview and presenting the best possible physical appearance are important, if not vital. The first few seconds of the interview are of prime importance. Many argue that decisions are often made at this time. A lot of things happen in a very short space of time:

- Entering the room.
- Seeing the interviewers for the first time.
- Waiting to be introduced.
- Maintaining eye contact.
- Giving each member of the interview team a firm handshake, if appropriate, and a warm smile.
- Sitting down when asked.
- Getting yourself seated as comfortably as possible.
- Trying not to lean too far forward or back and keeping your hands resting in your lap.

Listen carefully to the questions. Clarifying questions if necessary and answering clearly will help you make the right impression. Try to maintain eye contact with the interviewers when giving answers. Being nervous is fine but try to turn that nervousness into positive energy. Smiling as you wait helps relaxation. Sometimes, a little self-disclosure about yourself and how you are feeling can be helpful, but do not overdo it or you might appear weak. When people are nervous, they tend to speak faster than normal, so you may need to make a conscious effort to slow down your speech a little.

At the end of the meeting you will be asked if you have any questions. Have at least two or three prepared. These should be sensible, the last one being about when you are likely to hear the outcome of the interview. Sample questions at the end of the interview are:

- Where does the position fit into the company?
- Is there a performance appraisal system?
- Are there training and development opportunities?
- Are there any planned changes in products or services?

Express your deepening interest in the job, how it appeals to you and how you know you can achieve success in it.

Shake hands and thank each individual before you leave. Try not to dally too long, but do not rush.

## Educational Opportunities

Being made redundant can give you a chance to think about whether you would like to change career, develop new skills, recharge the batteries or move on to pastures new. Now is your time to do this. You might feel you need to return to further education. There are now many opportunities for adults to undertake a range of courses and training programmes, from acquiring basic skills to completing degree courses. These are accessible to and inclusive of all. The following are a few examples of what you might consider undertaking:

- Acquiring computer skills.
- Increasing your understanding of IT.
- Developing supervisory skills.
- Learning basic foreign language skills.
- Developing your ability to communicate.

These and more courses are available from the vocational education committees (VECs), FÁS, the institutes of technology, the National College of Ireland and the universities, if want to develop yourself further. AONTAS is the Irish national association for adult education. It has almost five hundred statutory and voluntary members, all of whom provide education opportunities.

Community education has developed strongly in recent years and it is estimated that there are over one thousand women's groups and a smaller number of men's groups providing learning and development opportunities to a diverse range of people. FÁS alone provides some four hundred courses annually throughout the country. They have a range of online courses whereby you can learn in your home environment and at your own pace.

Unemployed adults may be entitled to retain their benefits while attending a full-time third-level course in a university, institute of technology or other third-level institution. For adult learners attending courses that are approved by the Department of Education and Science for the Higher Education Grants Scheme, there are two principal forms of assistance:

- The Back to Education Allowance
- The Higher Education Grant

The Back to Education Allowance is an educational opportunities scheme for unemployed people, lone parents and people with disabilities who are getting certain payments from the Department of Social and Family Affairs. The Higher Education Grant is for mature students who are at least 23 years of age on 1 January of the year of entry or re-entry to an approved third-level course in an approved institution, and is subject to a means test.

Further education is a rewarding experience and will open doors to new opportunities, creating previously unreachable possibilities for the future. It will also help build your confidence, which may be flagging after redundancy.

## Setting Up Your Own Business

One of the options open to individuals who have been made redundant is to start their own business. First of all, you may have a lump sum to invest in any new venture. Secondly, there may be opportunities for your former employer to subcontract work out to you. Thirdly, you may have desired for a long time to become your own boss and have an idea that you would like to explore.

Before you start your own business, it is worth taking some time to look at your decision from all angles. Only then will you know you are making the right decision for you and your family. Starting your own business is a life-changing decision, and not just for you. Your family will be directly affected too. It is important to know up-front if your personality, life circumstances and finances are consistent with your dream of becoming your own boss and taking control of your own life.

*Personality traits*

Anyone can start a business. In fact there are nearly two hundred thousand businesses operating in Ireland. These range from large multinational companies to single-owner businesses with one person employed. Those who are successful tend to have a number of traits in common:

- Willingness to work hard.
- Belief in themselves and their product or service.
- Willingness to learn.
- Creative in problem solving.
- Resilient.
- Persistent.
- Pay attention to detail.

Other characteristics that are useful but which may be acquired from others include:

- Aptitude to understand and appreciate financial records and accounting procedures.
- Ability to understand basic legal requirements in relation to tax, employment, contracts, environment, and health and safety.

If you have only some of these characteristics, it is possible to find ways to compensate by additional training, partnering with someone else or hiring someone in. However, lacking in significant personality traits is likely to cause difficulties as the business gets started, and it may be prudent for your own and your family's well-being for you to remain an employee.

### Technical knowledge

Earlier in the chapter we looked at how to assess your capabilities. While it may not always be apparent, every business requires a level of technical knowledge. Whether you are in the retail trade or in the technical services area, absence of this knowledge could spell disaster.

It is important to assess exactly what key technical knowledge the business will require and to identify where your strengths and weaknesses lie.

### Practical business skills

Practical business skills are needed to succeed in business. No more than taking charge of a car without having some driving skills, the owner must have the basic skills to steer the business.

These skills essentially fall into two categories – administration and planning. Before setting up the business, a business plan is essential. The business plan will help you to think through the various elements that are required to make the business a success and what financing will be required. When preparing a business plan, make sure it is realistic. It is natural to be optimistic when starting out and this should be so. But being overly optimistic is what one has to be careful about. Banks have a rule of thumb when they receive plans from start-up promoters – they divide projected sales by two and multiply costs by two. This is based on long experience and should be heeded.

Getting help with a business plan is a very good idea. County enterprise boards, local chambers of commerce, banks, credit unions, FÁS and Enterprise Ireland are good sources of information and assistance.

A business plan can be a relatively simple document or quite detailed. This will depend on the complexity and size of the business and who you are trying to convince to support you. As a minimum, you will need to state the following:

- Nature and description of the business, including services or products being offered.
- A brief profile of the promoter(s), including track record.
- Objectives (in the form of turnover, number of customers, profitability and so on).
- Targeted customers.
- Who and what competitors there are.
- How you will achieve the sales.
- Why these customers will buy from you and not from others.
- Profit margins anticipated.
- What physical facilities you will need.
- A statement of sales, costs, profits or losses, and cash flows.
- Estimate of funding required to support the business, in detail over the first year and approximately for the subsequent year.

*Funding your business*

You may feel you have a great business idea and have the traits and abilities to be successful in business, but may not have the funding to do so. This means that you need to raise capital. First of all you will look at your personal savings and you may be able to enlist the support of family members or friends. There is also an array of business supports available. Support in the form of grant aid may be available from your local county enterprise board.

If it is an exportable service or product, you can look to Enterprise Ireland, Shannon Development or Údarás Na Gaeltachta, depending on the region in which the business will be located. Enterprise Ireland may also provide loans for suitable businesses in the form of preference shares or take direct equity participation. Business innovation centres provide support mechanisms for attracting private finance.

## Turning Redundancy into Advantage

Throughout this chapter the emphasis has been on treating redundancy as a life experience that can be turned into an advantage. Overcoming the initial shock, gathering all your facts and setting goals early on will give you the clarity and confidence to look ahead positively. Taking one step at a time and considering all your options will be far better in the medium term than rushing around without any sense of direction.

Thinking creatively about strategies to do this and enlisting the support of your family and friends will be helpful. Professional help is also available. Many people are shy of seeking such support but the returns can be enormous. Build on opportunities for development and growth. Take advantage of opportunities for training and development. Nurture your career so that you can make the most of your potential and achieve maximum personal satisfaction from your work life.

At different stages of life new priorities emerge. These demand that we adapt and change. It is never too late to change. Outside events, such as redundancy, can be triggers for such change. However, real change comes from within ourselves, not just from external events. Taking control of your life and the changes that you need to make is the best guarantee of future success and fulfilment.

# 11

# State Supports to Get You through the Slump

## Andrew McCann

In today's economic climate, in light of ever-increasing redundancies and unemployment, and the tightening of everyone's purse strings, it is even more important to know what financial supports are available to you and where to start looking. It is amazing the number of ways you can save money by reducing your tax bill, looking for a tax refund from the dreaded tax man, and finding out where you can get financial help in hard times. In this chapter I intend to look at three main areas of assistance:

1. What to do if or when you lose your job, and where to go for help.

2. Ways families can reduce their tax bill as well as avail of Government supports.

3. Assistance for the elderly: financial grants for house adaptation, medical cards for the over-seventies, and how to avoid paying tax if you are aged 65 or over.

**Losing Your Job – Where Do You Start?**

When you hear the dreaded news that you are being made redundant, this may be the first time in your life you have had to think about getting help from the State. You may not even know that help is available. So what do you do and where do you go? The first thing to know is that financial help is nearly always at hand if you have no money.

In assessing a case we must determine what is known as Pay-Related Social Insurance (PRSI) contributions. When you work and earn at least €38.09 per week, your employer generally pays a contribution (generally Class A) for you per week. If you are self-employed, you pay a different class of contribution, which entitles you to more limited benefits (Class S). Therefore, people who are employed make 52 contributions per year. (It is important therefore to fully examine your P60 – a document that your employer gives you at the end of each year, detailing all of the tax and PRSI deducted from your salary – and keep each one a safe place all your working life.)

There are a number of key questions to address in assessing any case:

- Did you leave your job of your own accord or was it due to conduct? If you left your job of your own accord you may be disqualified from receiving a payment for up to nine weeks.
- Did you receive a redundancy payment and, if so, how much? Payments of €50,000 or less from redundancy may be disregarded from your claim if you are not seeking a means-tested payment. Payments above €50,000 will be assessed on a case-by-case basis.
- How long (number of years) have you worked prior to losing your job? Social Welfare will look at what PRSI contributions you made two years prior to the date of

your current claim, i.e. Social Welfare will assess a claim made in 2009 with reference to contributions in either 2007 or 2006.

- Was the employer registered with Revenue and paying your social insurance contributions or were you paid cash-in-hand? Cash-in-hand payments, i.e. working in the 'black' economy, will only cover you for a means-tested payment.

- How much were your weekly earnings two years ago? Your average weekly wage two years prior to your claim will determine your weekly social welfare payment in some cases.

- Do you have a partner or spouse, is he or she working, how much is he or she earning and do you have any children? You may be eligible for a payment for a spouse or partner, even if they are working part-time.

- Have you recently only arrived or returned to Ireland? You must have been mainly (but not necessarily exclusively) living in Ireland for the last two years, even if you are an Irish citizen.

- Your age and residence (for instance, do you live at home with parents?). People aged 24 or under may have to be assessed on their parents' income if their only option is a means-tested payment.

- Were you self-employed or an employee? Self-employed people are not automatically entitled to a payment from their PRSI contributions, as they pay a different rate to employees.

When assessing your benefits, there are two types of payment possibly available to you: Jobseeker's Benefit or Jobseeker's Allowance. Jobseeker's Benefit claims are assessed purely on your previous contributions from paid employment in the two- or three-year period prior to your current claim. Therefore claims within 2009 will be determined by contributions made in either 2007 or 2006. In addition, since January 2009, you will be required to have a total of at least 104 contributions (at least two years' service) prior to making a claim. Also, to receive the maximum payment (€204.30 per week), you will need to have had at least an average weekly wage of €300 in the 'relevant' tax year, i.e. two to three years prior to your claim. In such cases a spouse or partner can earn up to €100 per week from employment without affecting your weekly payment for them. No payment is made for a spouse or partner if their earnings are above €300 per week, and in such cases you will only receive €13 per week for any dependent children.

---

### Number Crunch

In January 2009, the number of people claiming Jobseeker's Benefit or Allowance stood at **328,000**. Just one year earlier, the total number of claimants on the live register stood at **181,000**, meaning that, in the space of just 12 months, the number of people who were forced by recession to hit the dole queues soared by **80 per cent**. The surge in claimants in January 2009 was the highest on record in Ireland to date.

---

Jobseeker's Allowance claims (means-tested) are purely assessed on your savings and/or your spouse or partner's income. As a single person, you may have at least €20,000 in savings and still receive a payment. A married couple (couples cohabiting are assessed in a similar way to married couples) can have at least €40,000 in savings and still receive a payment (it is assumed money in a joint account is divided 50:50). Income from a spouse or partner is assessed depending on the number of days they work, and only at 60 per cent of their income (subject to the maximum payment due based on the size of your dependent family). Self-employed persons are assessed

128

differently and their means (assessable income) is determined as their average income over the previous 12-month period.

So what do you do and how do you know which payment you will receive? The first thing to do is to visit your local social welfare office as soon as you lose your job, because your claim will only start from the day you visit your local office. You will also lose the first three days of your claim. You will need to bring the following documents with you:

- P45 or a letter from your employer stating you have ceased employment.
- Birth certificate, passport or proof of ID (picture ID).
- Personal public service (PPS) number (formerly PRSI number).
- Household utility bill (with your name on it).
- A letter from FÁS stating you have registered with them.

To be eligible to receive either payment, you must be:

- Unemployed.
- Aged under 66.
- Be capable of working, available for and genuinely seeking full-time work.
- Have a substantial loss of employment, i.e. you are un-employed for at least three out of six consecutive days (social welfare claims are from Monday to Saturday).

The Department of Social and Family Affairs will be able to investigate whether or not you are eligible for either a Jobseeker's Benefit or Allowance payment (depending on your circumstances). The maximum weekly payment for a claimant is €204.30 per week, €135.60 for a qualified adult (spouse or partner), and a maximum of €26 per child (up to a maximum age of 22, in full-time education).

*So, what other help is available?*

Help with your rent or mortgage

Help is available with your rent or the interest part of the mortgage only. Help with your rent will be determined by the size of your dependent family, subject to maximum rent thresholds set across the country. In addition, assistance with your rent or the interest part of your mortgage is assessed subject to your income from employment (the first €75 per week of earnings is exempt, as well as 25 per cent of the balance of your income from employment), maintenance payments (subject to the amount received), or other social welfare payments over and above the set minimum amount payable for your family size. Assistance is not provided if you work full-time, which is defined as more than 30 hours per week. In addition, you will have to pay a 'housing element' at €18 per week per adult.

To seek assistance you will need to visit your local community welfare officer. You will be required to complete an application form and provide supporting documentation (which may include you submitting an application to your local city or county council for social housing). You will also be required to provide either a copy of your lease or a statement from your lending institution showing the proportion of loan or interest paid as part of your monthly mortgage.

Help with 'one-off' bills

The community welfare officer may also be able to assist you under the Urgent or Exceptional Needs Payment Scheme. This payment scheme is at the discretion of the community welfare officer for one-off bills and is assessed on a case-by-case basis.

## As a Family, How Can You Reduce Your Tax Bill as well as Gain Extra Benefits?

As a family, you need to consider how you can reduce your tax bill as well as identify additional financial supports available to you.

*Taxation*

How do you know if you are paying too much tax? The first consideration should be whether you are claiming all the tax credits available to you. The tax system is administered differently to the social welfare system. The tax system either sees you as single or married, and does not treat cohabiting couples the same as married persons (as the social welfare system does). You can look to backdate any claim for a maximum of four years, i.e. claims from at least 2005 onwards. You can download the forms mentioned below from the website of the Revenue Commissioner or you can apply online by registering with PAYE Anytime (www.revenue.ie). Some of the more common underutilised tax credits are as follows:

Single-income families

As a single-income family, if your spouse is at home minding the children or a child with a permanent physical or mental disability, or caring for a person aged 65 or over residing with you (or in close proximity), the main earner may be entitled to an additional tax credit known as a Home Carer's Tax Credit. This is an additional €900 per year, and is equivalent to an extra €4,500 of tax-free earnings. In addition, the home carer may be able to work part-time (and earn up to a maximum of €5,080) and still receive a reduced Home Carer's Tax Credit.

### Rent relief

Do you know you can gain additional tax credits if you are renting? By simply completing a RENT1 form (even without your landlord's PPS details) you can seek to claim relief on the rent you pay to a private landlord (payment to a parent is excluded). As a single person this can create savings of €2,000 per year tax free (if you are under age 55), and up to €4,000 for a married couple. These figures are doubled if you are over 55 and/or married.

### Single parent tax relief

As a single parent you may be aware you can receive additional tax credits whilst parenting alone, but are you aware you can receive additional tax credits if you, as a supporting parent, have your child/ren over to stay? This additional relief is not available to cohabiting couples (even if you are not living with your child). To apply, simply fill in an OP1 form. This is worth a tax-free earning of €9,150 per year.

### Dependent relatives

If you are looking after a dependent relative (someone old or infirm) at your own expense and their income is below €12,745 per year, you may be eligible to an additional tax credit of €80 per year. Such dependent relatives may include your relatives or your spouse's relatives. A DR2 form is required.

### Medical expenses

Do you know you can look to claim back expenses on your prescriptions, doctor and specialist bills, hospital stays and nursing home fees in relation to a close relative? Prior to 2009, you could claim medical expenses back at the higher tax bracket (41 per cent if you were taxed on that rate). Claims in relation to 2009 can only be made at the lower tax bracket (20 per cent) with the exception of nursing home fees, which are still claimable at the higher bracket of 41 per cent for 2009 only. From 2010, all medical expenses will be claimable at the lower bracket only. Since 2007 there is no minimum threshold for claims (all medical expenses claimable). Medical expenses may even include medical equipment and accommodation (if healthcare is only available outside the State or if, as a parent, you have to stay with a child overnight (certain medical conditions only)). Claims made in relation to the years prior to 2007 require a deduction of €125 for a single person and €250 for a married couple. Expenses can also be claimed for dental expenses (even if such work takes place in another country). You cannot claim for routine work (scaling, extraction, fillings).

Rent-a-Room Scheme

In difficult financial times, you may want to consider renting out a room in your house. You can receive rent to a maximum of €10,000 per year tax free (€192.31 per week) but, if you exceed this amount, all income is taxable at 20 per cent. Income from a Rent-a-Room Scheme must be declared to Revenue. This scheme is not available if the person renting the room is a family member.

Other tax reliefs available include those on the costs of refuse collection (up to a maximum of €80 tax credit per year), union subscriptions (maximum of €70 tax credit per year) and tuition fees (maximum of 20 per cent of fees up to €5,000 per year, i.e. a €1,000 tax credit). To claim your tax credits, please contact your local tax office.

Family Income Supplement

Family Income Supplement is a top-up payment for families on low incomes (including single parents). To be eligible, you must work at least 19 hours per week (or 38 hours in a fortnight), have at least one dependent child and be under the set income threshold (net pay) for your family size. All income is taken into account (including the majority of social welfare payments). The Family Income Supplement is assessed as 60 per cent of the difference between the income threshold (for your family size) and your net income. The minimum payment is at least €20 per week and, once assessed, payments are made for 52 weeks (regardless of whether you receive a pay increase). The income limit for a family with one child is €500, €590 for two children, €685 for three children and €800 for four children.

### Medical card and GP card

Contrary to some opinions, medical and GP cards are available to working families. Medical cards cover GP visits, prescribed medication and hospital stays, whereas the GP card only covers GP visit costs. Although the income thresholds are low for families – at €266.50 per week (medical card) and €400 per week (GP card) for a married couple – these thresholds can be increased depending on the number of children you have – by €38 per child (medical card) and €57 per child (GP card). Thresholds are also dependent on the number of children you have, their ages and whether or not they receive a college grant. On the positive side, all expenditure on rent or a mortgage is fully taken into account, as well as a maximum €50 weekly payment towards a car loan, or travel costs to or from work (this rate will vary if you work unsocial hours). Also, all reasonable childcare costs are considered, including payments to crèches, child minders and family members. Be aware that payments to family members may affect their other social welfare payments.

Finally, even if you are outside the income threshold, medical and GP cards may be awarded dependent on certain medical conditions. Long-term illness cards (regardless of income) are also available to certain people who are diagnosed with certain medical conditions.

If you have been unemployed for 12 months (and getting a social welfare payment) and return to work, you can seek to retain your medical card for up to three years (regardless of your income) under the Retention Scheme.

*Support for one-parent families*

As a single parent (i.e. separated or divorced for three months or more, or parenting alone), you can seek the One-Parent Family Payment from the Department of Social and Family Affairs if your weekly income from employment is less than €425 per week (minimum weekly payment granted), and you are the main person looking after your child/ren. If your income from employment is €146.50 per week or less, you keep all your One-Parent Family Payment (€204.30 per week and €26 per child). Income from employment over and above €146.50 is halved (up to the maximum of €425 per week) and assessed against a tapered scale (subject to your income).

The One-Parent Family Payment is not available to couples cohabiting, regardless if any children residing with them are from the current or a past relationship. In addition, people seeking a One-Parent Family Payment are requested to seek maintenance from the father of the child/ren. The maintenance recovery section of the One-Parent Family Department may also seek maintenance payments from the other parent if they are not currently financially supporting their child, or if the department believes the rate of maintenance being paid is below a reasonable threshold. Income from maintenance is taken into account when assessing your weekly payment. However, if you are receiving at least €95.23 per week in maintenance, you may be able to disregard such income from your assessment if you have to pay rent or a mortgage for your accommodation in excess of this threshold.

You can also seek the Family Income Supplement (as discussed earlier) on top of your One-Parent Family Payment (subject to your means). You may also seek an extra half-rate Jobseeker's Benefit payment (as discussed earlier) or an extra half-rate Illness Benefit (if you cannot work due to illness and have the appropriate contributions) in addition to your One-Parent Family Payment.

## What Supports Are Available to the Elderly?

So what supports are available to the elderly to adapt their homes, how will the new medical card thresholds for the over-seventies affect you, and how do you ensure you're free from tax and exempt from DIRT tax on your savings?

### Housing aids for older people

This scheme was introduced on 1 November 2007 and is a means-tested scheme for (but not exclusive to) those aged 60 or over. The scheme covers such work as structural repairs, re-wiring, replacement of doors and windows, bathroom adaptation, and heating. If your earnings are less than €30,000 per year, you may be entitled to the full grant of €10,500. If you earn over the threshold and up to a maximum of €65,000 per year, you can even receive a reduced grant of €3,150. This scheme is administered by your local city or county council. The grant must be approved prior to the commencement of any work.

## Medical cards (over-seventies)

Under the Budget 2009 changes, a new means-tested scheme is now in operation since January 2009. The income threshold for a single person is €700 per week (gross earnings) and €1,400 (gross) for a married couple. In addition, the savings disregard is €36,000 for a single person and €72,000 for a married couple (no deductions are applicable). Savings over these thresholds are assessed on the weekly interest income earned (dependent on the interest rate given to you by your financial institution) and added to your gross weekly income. Even if you are over the income thresholds, you may still wish to include any relevant medical conditions in support of your case. You may even request to be assessed on medical grounds only (excluding the means test). If one spouse is under 70 and the other spouse is over 70, the new higher thresholds will apply. If you already held a medical card (if you are over 70) prior to 1 January 2009, you will be required to complete an income assessment if your income is above the new threshold. If in such circumstances your income exceeds the threshold eligible for a medical card, you can apply on the basis of medical care needs. Such applications are then only assessed on the medical need rather than the financial eligibility.

If a couple is under 70, the normal means test threshold will apply (€298 per week for a married couple (medical card) and €447 for a married couple (GP Card)). This savings threshold is assessed differently to the over-seventies scales. For single or married people under 70 the savings thresholds exclude the first €20,000 for a single person and €40,000 for a married couple. Savings above such thresholds are assessed on a tapered basis: thresholds increase as the savings increase.

*Sit Tight and Get It Right*

Marginal Tax Relief and Deposit Interest Retention Tax (DIRT)

If you are over 65 (single or married), you may wish to be assessed under the Marginal Tax Relief Scheme. What this means is that, if your income is less than €20,000 per year (single person) and less than €40,000 (married), you can be exempt from the tax system. If your income is above these thresholds, you may wish to have your tax affairs assessed at the marginal rate (40 per cent) for income above the threshold, or assessed through the normal tax credit system. If you are exempt from the tax system, you can apply for an exemption from DIRT Tax on your savings. To do so, you need to complete a DE1 form. If you are permanently incapacitated, you can apply for an exemption from DIRT Tax also (by completing a DE2 form). Of course you can seek to backdate your claim to at least 2005.

If you are exempt from tax, you may also be eligible to seek an exemption from refuse charges from your local or city council. You will be required to complete an application form and return it accordingly to your local authority.

Age Tax Credit

If you are still within the tax system and do not wish to be assessed at the marginal tax rate, you can seek an additional Age Tax Credit (at age 65). The tax credit is €325 for a single person and €650 for a married couple. This equates to a tax saving of €1,625 per year for a single person and €3,250 for a married person.

**Summary**

So, as you can see, if you are new to the social welfare system, that is, you have just become unemployed and/or

138

your family is struggling to survive, or if you are in your mature years and looking to save money, there are numerous options available to you, subject to your financial situation. This chapter only briefly examines some of the tax reliefs and social welfare supports available to you. For further information, check out *Know Your Rights* (2009 edition), or contact your local Citizens Information Centre (www.citizensinformation.ie), or the national Citizens Information Centre network (lo-call 1890 777 121).

# 12

# Dicing With Debt

## Caroline Madden and Laura Slattery

After the credit binge comes the debt hangover. One day you're merrily (and instinctively) punching in your PIN at the shop counter and gleefully embracing those terribly thoughtful 'buy now, pay later' deals at the furniture store, the next day you're shuddering as you try to work out if your current account has got enough cash in it to make those minimum monthly repayments. What's 5 per cent of €10,000 anyway?

Oh.

That's when you start to think it might be a good idea to take out another credit card – you know, something nice and platinum-hued, just to keep the gold one in your wallet company. Not because you're going to need it to pay for such prosaic things as food and electricity while you use your overdraft to pay off those older debts you had hoped would just go away.

But what's this? Ah, a leaflet showing you how you can reduce your monthly repayments if you roll all your debts into one easy loan. 'Where do I sign?' you ask. And while you're at it, why not apply for another €20k. There's no harm in asking. Those kitchen cabinets have been looking

# Sit Tight and Get It Right

a bit grubby for a while now. That car in your driveway is
rusting in all the wrong places. And to round off your dive
into 'I deserve it' debt, you mentally set aside an extra
couple of grand of money you haven't earned for that
dream holiday. It's not a proper break if you haven't
crossed at least five time zones and come back with
enough different currencies to open a bureau de change.

That was the old you. The new you knows when the time
is right to put the plastic away, give your credit card a cath-
artic chop and avoid the temptation to slot the fragments
together again for some last-hurrah online purchases.
Your repayment burden is heavy enough, thank you.

And even if you haven't yet been moved to join the 'buy
now, pay now' brigade, the chances are that your kind
sponsors – the banks – will soon force your hand. This
recession has coincided with (and been partly caused by)
a crisis of confidence in the global financial system known
as the credit crunch. Essentially, the crunch struck after
US 'subprime' mortgage lenders gave trillions to people
who couldn't afford to pay it back. The lenders then
parcelled up the debt and sold it on to other financial
institutions. When the money had to be written off as
'toxic assets', suddenly mistrustful banks were no longer
willing or able to lend money to other banks. Without
these regular flows of inter-bank finance, some banks left
themselves a bit short of cash to lend to borrowers.

The upshot of the subprime debacle and the credit
crunch is that lenders will probably be much choosier
when it comes to rubber-stamping loan applications. So,
whether you're trying to clear your debts, having trouble
meeting your repayments or hoping to borrow fresh credit,
it's a tricky time. But whatever it is you're trying to do,
there are steps you can take to make the road to a
credit-boosted budget or – whisper it – a debt-free existence
that bit less rocky.

142

## Credit Where Credit Is Due (and Sometimes Where it Isn't)

Okay, so what do you do in these credit crunch times when you're looking to borrow money?

Much will depend on the reason why you're tapping these poor cash-strapped banks for the few coins they've got left in the first place. Maybe you're a humble first-time buyer hoping to call the bottom of the housing market. Maybe you've got one of those recession-proof jobs like corporate insolvency expert or bike manufacturer. Or perhaps you're simply an unrepentant credit junkie who didn't get the memo that told everyone that debt-fuelled extravagance is just *so* 2007.

Whatever your motivation, here are our seven steps to sensible borrowing in the slump:

### 1. Protect your credit rating

In pre-crunch days, financial institutions were all too happy to lend money to people with patchy credit records, seeing it as a delightful opportunity to charge higher interest rates on the grounds that less-than-perfect borrowers posed extra 'risk' to their fragile balance sheets. But now that banks are far more picky about their choice of customer, you must strive even harder to keep your credit rating fully intact. If you've got existing debt, this means doing everything you can to make the repayments; and, if you're applying for a loan, this means taking extra special care not to borrow so much that you damage your good standing. Blot your credit history and you could find it next to impossible to secure a loan in the future – when you might really need it.

### 2. Get saving

It might seem kind of crazy, but the first thing you should do if you want to borrow money is start doing the exact opposite: save. 'But if I could afford to put money aside in a savings account each month, I probably wouldn't need to borrow the cash in the first place,' you might say. That's true, and it's also a sad fact that the rate of interest that you will earn on your savings will often be lower than the rate you are charged on your borrowings.

However, with recession sparking so many redundancies, being in hock can be dangerous. You can take out expensive payment protection insurance (PPI) that covers the loan repayments for a temporary period if you do lose your job, but the smarter thing to do is to self-insure yourself with a 'rainy day' fund that will keep your finances ticking over if you're out of work for a while. With the days of 100 per cent mortgages swept away by the credit crunch, saving has also regained its importance for potential first-time buyers, who may be asked to stump up a deposit of as much as 20 per cent.

### 3. Give yourself a stress test

A financial stress test is a precautionary step that lenders are supposed to conduct on your behalf before they hand you a mortgage cheque. In practice, it involves checking to see if you could still afford the repayments should interest rates increase in the years after you draw down the debt. But you can do your own, more encompassing stress test. Start by forensically examining your employment contract. What kind of job security do you have? Are there layoffs occurring elsewhere in your sector? If you're stuck in a lift with the human resources director, stare him or her directly in the eyes to see if he or she knows something you don't. Interest rates may be falling rather than rising, but no amount of rate cuts are going to help you make your mortgage repayments if you lose your job.

## 4. Window shop

In our more spendthrift, credit-loving days, lenders used to stuff our letterboxes with leaflets telling us that we had been 'pre-approved' for all manner of unsolicited loans, and sometimes we said 'okay, then' to their very kind offers and hotfooted it to the nearest retail park. Now the Financial Regulator has banned lenders from offering 'pre-approved' anything, so the onus is on would-be borrowers to shop around for their credit. Check as many lenders as you can before borrowing, as the cost of credit can vary wildly. Remember that it's not just banks and building societies that offer loans: your local or workplace credit union may be a source of short-term loans, while your local authority will have details of any State-assisted mortgages for which you might qualify.

## 5. Avoid the wrong kind of debt

Before you borrow a cent, you should be at least vaguely aware of the different types of credit and the appropriate way to use them. Firstly, credit cards are suitable for short-term borrowing only. Around half of all cardholders repay their full balances every month within the interest-free period on the card. Join the club and don't spend more on your card than you can afford to repay with your following month's salary. Beware that if you sign up to 'forecourt finance', i.e. you buy a car using a credit deal offered by the garage, it is usually a hire purchase (HP) contract, which means you don't technically own the car until you make the final repayment. Remember that your mortgage is secured on your home. If you can't repay it, your home could be repossessed. Don't use the equity in your home as a slush fund to withdraw from via a mortgage top-up whenever you feel like a holiday. Strictly speaking, mortgage top-ups should only be used to make home improvements that will add to the value of your property.

> ### Number Crunch
>
> Credit card indebtedness in Ireland rose at a rate of almost **20 per cent** in the year to March 2007. But since those feverish days, our fondness for splashing out on plastic has dimmed. In January 2009, outstanding indebtedness on credit cards was growing at the much calmer annual rate of **4 per cent**. But our collective monthly bill on personal credit cards still exceeded a staggering **€2.9 billion**, while we totted up new spending of almost **€870 million**.

### 6. Be honest

You may be tempted to treat your loan application form like a CV and brashly overstate your vital statistics – in this case, your income and your savings – in a bid to get what you want. But you won't score any marks for lying. In today's crunch-bitten times, lenders will be taking extra special care to examine your payslips and your current account balance with a magnifying glass and a hard heart before deciding whether or not to give you the loan. If you are successful in inventing non-existent income or hiding existing debts and manage to convince lenders that you're good for the money, you will automatically be exposing yourself to more debt than you can afford. As the saying goes, the only person you will be hurting is yourself.

### 7. Do take no for an answer

Rejection is hard, but sometimes it's a good idea to just take it and move on. All lenders have different lending policies at different times, so while one bank might give you a flat 'no' to your loan application and another credit card provider might laugh in your face if you ask for a €15,000 credit limit, the bank or card provider across the street might be only too happy for your custom. However, if it seems like every financial institution in Ireland is ignoring your desperate pleas for cash, it might just be for a reason: it's not them, it's *you*. If the credit you want is for an optional 'lifestyle' purchase, the best thing to do is to wait until your income rises or lenders become more generous again. If you are seeking a loan because your income isn't high enough to pay your month-to-month bills, you have a much bigger problem. Being turned down for a loan could still be a blessing in disguise: rather than adding to your financial woes by trapping you in a cycle of debt, it may force you to seek help.

## Back to Black: How to Achieve a Debt-Free Lifestyle

It's one of life's cruel ironies that racking up debts is as easy as falling off a log, but paying them back is like pulling teeth – slow and painful. Perhaps this is why it's so tempting to chuck credit card statements into the recycling bin unopened and shove unpaid bills to the back of a drawer. But you can't postpone the inevitable forever. If you want to keep the wolf from the door and the roof over your head, sooner or later you have to face the music and start paying back all those nasty debts that you've somehow accumulated.

The secret to clearing debt is to take out your magic wand and wave it over a pile of bank statements ... we wish. Unfortunately there is no magic solution to make all of your debts and creditors instantly disappear, be they overdraft or overdue bills, credit card or credit union, pushy pin-striped bankers or shifty sheepskin-coated loan sharks. The most effective approach to ditching debt is far more mundane.

The key lies in rediscovering the lost art of living within your means. In order to do this you must familiarise yourself with what your 'means' actually are. The only way to find this out – dull as it may sound – is by budgeting. Work out a monthly budget, listing your income and all your outgoings. It may make you wince, but be honest. You'll immediately see whether you should have a nice dollop of disposable income left over at the end of each month, or whether belts need to be tightened and luxuries foregone in order to avoid overspending and to free up some cash.

Next, list all of your debts, from 'secured' debts such as a mortgage, which is tied to your home, to unsecured 'lifestyle' debts like credit and store card bills. Don't forget to include hire purchase debts, personal loans, overdrafts and any unpaid utility bills. Then decide which debts should take priority. Think about the consequences of getting into arrears on each of your debts. For example, if you don't pay your electricity bills, it's only a matter of time before you'll be digging out the candles; if your mortgage payments are overdue, you risk losing your home; and if you fail to pay certain fines, you could even end up in the clink.

Work out how much you can afford to pay to each of your priority creditors each month, and be disciplined in sticking to this, even if it means making fairly drastic cutbacks to your lifestyle. Once you have your priority debts under control, work out a programme for chipping away steadily at your secondary (less urgent) debts, targeting the most expensive, short-term borrowings first.

With credit cards (which tend to have some of the highest interest rates around), you must make more than the minimum repayments if you ever want to get to the bottom of your debt. Also, consider switching the balance owed on your existing card to a new provider offering a 0 per cent introductory rate.

Your mortgage may seem like an insurmountable debt mountain that you expect to be still trying to scale when you're old and grey, but there are clever ways of reducing the lifetime of your home loan and saving thousands in interest repayments. If, for example, interest rates are cut further, instead of pocketing the savings, maintain your mortgage repayments at the previous higher level.

Or if you have enough wriggle room in your budget, consider overpaying your mortgage, for example, by making one extra payment a year. (If you have a fixed-rate mortgage, you will have less flexibility in pursuing this strategy and other mortgage-related strategies mentioned in this chapter). But make sure to check that the overpayments go towards paying off the principal on the loan.

If you find yourself with a lump sum, whether from savings or a windfall, consider using some of it to knock a hole in your mortgage. One argument against this is that it's possible that you could get a higher return on your lump sum if you invested it, for example, in the stock market. However, as recent events have proven, this is not without its risks.

Once you have achieved that elusive state of being debt-free, or have at least gained control over your borrowings, here's a very retro idea to consider: why not resolve to live without relying on credit? Think about it: no sleepless nights worrying whether the heavies will turn up on your doorstep in the morning and make off with your beloved flat-screen TV tucked under their brawny arms; and more disposable income now that you're not wasting money on unnecessary interest repayments. You'll be in a stronger position to withstand whatever the economy may throw at you, and of course there's the superior feeling that comes with kicking the credit habit. Here are a few tips to avoid slipping back into your old credit-fuelled lifestyle:

- Get the scissors out: you may have had some great times together, but now it's time for you and your flexible friends to go your separate ways. Don't just lock your credit and store cards away in a safe – chop them up into tiny pieces. From now on cash is king, but if you must have some plastic in your wallet, make it a debit or laser card – if your account is bare, it won't work.
- You might want to consider – brace yourself – *saving up* for big-ticket items that you really want. True, you could have that three-piece suite now if you signed up for the tempting in-store finance offer, but then you'd be right back on the slippery debt slope and it would probably cost you more in the long run. And think of it this way, if you have to save up first you'll be far less likely to make regrettable impulse buys, and you may actually come to appreciate your belongings far more than in the 'easy come, easy go' boom times.
- Forget about keeping up with the Joneses. Flashing the cash is now considered a sign of serious bad taste, which should make it easier for reformed credit bingers to stay on the straight and narrow.

**Dealing with Debt Difficulties**

Bills covered in angry red writing are piling up. The repo man has threatened to take back belongings that you bought on the never-never. You've resorted to tapping friends and family for loans, convincing them (and quite possibly yourself) that you just have a temporary cash-flow problem. The truth is you're caught in a debt trap and you can't see any way out.

The most important thing is to face up to the seriousness of the situation and to seek help – now. The Money Advice and Budgeting Service (www.mabs.ie) provides free, confidential advice to people with serious debt problems. MABS have at least one office in every county in Ireland, so contact your nearest office immediately.

It's also important to accept that there is no shame in getting into debt. It happens to the best of people, and is very often caused not by reckless spending, but by events beyond their control, for example, an illness or death in the family or losing their job.

Budgeting and prioritising your creditors (as outlined in the section above) become critical if you're in financial difficulty. There are a number of other issues to consider when trying to escape the debt spiral:

### 1. Contact your creditors

If you are struggling with loan repayments or have already fallen into arrears, contact your creditors to let them know. A sample letter is available on www.mabs.ie.

Explain the reason for any missed payments, and ask them for some breathing space. Be upfront and honest – explain that you're in financial difficulty and send them a realistic budget showing how much you can afford to pay each week or month. If you're back on track with your regular monthly repayments, but can't afford to catch up on arrears immediately, ask them to be flexible about this. For example, suggest that they let you spread the missed payment over the next few payments.

The good news is that most lenders are far more interested in finding a mutually agreeable solution than pursuing borrowers through the courts.

## 2. Maximise your income

Is there any way that you could increase your income? Are you claiming your full tax and social welfare entitlements? Could you rent out a room in your house to help pay the mortgage? Could you take a second job?

## 3. Check for protection

If you took out payment protection insurance with a loan, then the loan repayments may be temporarily covered if you had an accident, suffered an illness or were made redundant. Make sure to check any such policy to see if you can make a claim.

## 4. Think twice before consolidating your debt

'Roll all your debts into one easy payment!' Sounds like the answer to all your money woes, doesn't it? But before you fall for one of these ads, bear in mind that, while consolidating all of your debts into one loan (or rolling them up into your mortgage) may result in lower monthly repayments, over the life of the loan it's likely to cost you more. Also, if your debt consolidation loan is secured against your home, then if you miss the repayments on that loan your home could be at risk.

## 5. Don't borrow from Peter to pay Paul

Don't be tempted to resort to more extreme 'solutions', for example, using credit cards and loans to cover your mortgage bill. Using expensive short-term credit to service a mortgage in this way only compounds the problem; if you're in a hole, stop digging. Think about it: does borrowing your way out of debt make sense?

### 6. Ask for a mortgage holiday

One very simple, albeit temporary, solution if you're struggling to meet your mortgage repayments is to arrange a mortgage payment holiday, or moratorium, for a period of three to six months. This break could well give you the breathing space that you need – perhaps to find a new job if you've been laid off – and to get back on track. Remember that repayments may be higher after the break.

Use it as an opportunity to save hard and make the necessary cutbacks in your lifestyle so that you won't fall back into the same rut as soon as the repayments resume.

### 7. Extend the life of your mortgage

It may be possible to negotiate a longer loan term with your mortgage lender, for example, extending a 20-year mortgage to a 25- or 30-year term. This option will make your mortgage bill more affordable and give you some wriggle room in your monthly budget.

### Time for a Debt Detox

Whether you're a first-time borrower or a reformed debt-aholic, the key to financial security is keeping your reliance on debt to a minimum. There is very little any of us can do about external financial forces like interest rates, bank lending policies or liquidity crises, but we *can* insulate ourselves by reducing our dependency on debt. After all, if the credit crunch has taught us anything it's that dicing with debt is a dangerous game.

# 13

# Investors in a Dangerous Time

## Ian Mitchell

I'd escaped from the office early one evening in summer 2008, worn out by what in retrospect transpired to be one of the first harsh breezes of the oncoming credit crunch tsunami, when my mobile began to bleep in my pocket.

*IAN, IS THE WRLD IN REAL BIG TRUBLE? SHOULD WE SELL OUR HOUSE & RENT A SMALL PLACE? How r u n e way? Xx*

She's an actress – that explained the melodrama. She was afraid – that explained the capital letters. And even back then she spoke for a lot of people. I took more than a moment to respond.

You probably remember those balmy days when experts were lining up to tell us that things might not be too bad. There was a bandying about of words like 'correction' and phrases like 'soft landing'. No one back then had learned to spell 'recession' and depression was a Tiger-generated status symbol choreographed by your therapist. Predicted recovery in early 2009 was a common fiction of the times.

Just before leaving the office that day I'd met with two youthful Northern 'property entrepreneurs', just back from Barbados of all places, where they'd been trying to entice developers into dumping apartments onto the Irish market en bloc at what back then had seemed like fire sale prices. After factoring in 15 per cent for the boys of course – that kind of fire sale.

Ah, lads, if only it had been that simple.

We were, of course, beginning to hear quite a lot about the credit crunch, and from all kinds of unlikely people. In the media the term was becoming ubiquitous in its all-pervading, all-explaining power. Back then the credit crunch was becoming like God – pretty much omnipotent and omnipresent; the causal force behind every inexplic-able event. Like why the cost of sandwiches was rising in the coffee shop beside the office. Or why the noises coming out of investment bank Lehman were disturbing.

Judging by the people enjoying the June sunshine and surveying a sculpture exhibition in the park that day, Nietzsche was right about God being dead; well, in her credit-crunch incarnation anyway. There were a lot of seriously well-heeled people sipping complimentary champagne; you might say it seemed to be a genuinely crunch-free space. I wondered for a moment if I ought to ring the coffee shop about their sandwich price policy.

Six months later, at the time of writing this chapter, my actor friend is still living in her house and I'm still working out an adequate response to her first question. The one about the world being in 'real big trouble'. I've sat through a lot of presentations by a lot of experts – investment fund managers, economists, pension scheme trustees and corporate CEOs, to categorise but a few – and I'm convinced that they're trying to work out their responses too. Instinctively, I feel that the answer is yes.

And if the answer to her question about the world being in trouble is still yes – and just about all of the informed opinion that I have listened to as 2008 wore thin would appear to be in agreement that it is – and if we are looking out towards late 2010 or even 2011 as being the time when economic life reverts to behaving in a way that we might begin to call normal, then we need to think very carefully about where we should invest whatever cash that we might have at our disposal.

And when I think about investment strategies in these financially dangerous times, the first thing that comes to mind is the notion of *investing to minimise risk*.

All of us have areas of financial risk in our lives, whether it is our maxed-out credit cards, or the buy-to-let we bought in late 2007, or the fact that our job is in a sector too closely aligned to the banking or construction sectors to allow us to sleep easy at night, or that we're reliant on our investment income to help us pay our bills. We all learned to take risks back in the Tiger years, and then events moved too swiftly to allow many of us to plan our way to safety.

But if we have a job then we have an income stream; and if we have an income stream then we have a potential roadmap to help us reach the relative financial safety of a risk-reduced lifestyle. And a risk-reduced lifestyle can become the bedrock from which we may be able to take advantage of an economic upturn when it eventually comes along.

### So, How Do We Invest to Reduce Risk?

1. Well, we should start with our most obvious area of vulnerability: our short-term debts. The interest levied on unsettled credit card debt is still at double-digit levels, and this in a time when international bank

base rates are probably going to levels as low or lower than they have been in our lifetime. It should be our first investment priority to put aside enough money to free ourselves from these and other short-term personal loans, such as hire purchase agreements and car purchase finance. That way we have established ownership over the items we used the monies to purchase and eliminated the risk of being unable to keep up future payments with the resultant exposure to court action and/or repossession of any articles purchased through the finance.

2. Once we've done that we should have a look at our mortgage position – particularly if we purchased a property at the 2007 price peaks by utilising a relatively high loan-to-value mortgage. The risk in maintaining this high mortgage is of course that we might find ourselves in negative equity as house prices continue to fall and, whilst negative equity is not a particularly dangerous phenomenon as long as we are able to make the required repayments, it does have some unpleasant potential side effects if, for instance, we were to become unemployed, or indeed if we wished to apply for another job in a location that would make it necessary to relocate. So it does make sense for anyone with funds to invest to try to bring their mortgage amount down to as close to 80 per cent of the current value of their home as possible. That way you do have some slack in the system in the event of an emergency, and have also kept your location options open.

3. All of which leads me to the next priority, which is to invest as much as possible in a contingency fund – a

reasonably decent interest-bearing account in a bank or building society, requiring no more than 30 days' notice in order to make withdrawals. I'd recommend that we aim to retain in such an easy access fund enough cash to fund our lifestyle for a six-month period in the event that our, or our partner's, job becomes a casualty of the economic times in which we live. It is also vital that some of our investments are held in such a way that, if we do have an urgent need for cash, we can obtain access within a one- to three-month period.

4. One huge area of risk that has been highlighted in the media during 2008 is that created within pension schemes by the unprecedented fall in equity values. There's been a lot of carnage out there in 'pension world' and many managed funds (in which the significant majority of us invest our monthly or annual pension contributions) have fallen by as much as 35 per cent over the year. This has raised some very important questions in the minds of many people who are relying on these pension plans to ensure that their bills are paid in retirement.

### Number Crunch

The ravages of world equity markets wiped a staggering **€27 billion** from Irish pension funds in 2008. The group pension funds managed by investment experts on behalf of company pension schemes lost an average of more than one-third of their value during the turbulent year, leaving many company schemes with massive deficits. Meanwhile, almost half of workers do not have any pension savings and may have to rely on the State pension for retirement income.

**So, How Can We Ensure that We Invest in Such a Way as to Minimise Risk in Our Pension Plans?**

1. First of all, we need to understand that perhaps, for many of us, the biggest 'wins' of all in pension planning are the contributions made on our behalf by other people. For those of us who are members of a company pension scheme, a significant part of the monthly or annual contribution is made by our employer and by Revenue. In many schemes, these two parties combine to contribute as much as 71.5 per cent of what goes in. Thus it's vital that the scheme member doesn't put all this extra contribution at unnecessary risk through her or his investment decisions.

2. It's a fact not widely appreciated that almost every pension provider allows scheme members to move their investments between a number of various investment funds free of charge and on a fairly generous basis. The value of this is that we, as pension savers, are not locked into the, possibly quite uninformed, choices that we made when we joined the scheme. And we can move our past savings or redirect our future savings into investment environments that better suit either our own individual risk tolerance levels, or indeed the financial circumstances in which we find ourselves at a particular time. This is a very useful benefit in a time like this.

3. My own view about pension savings is this: if I can put €28.50 each month into an account, and then someone else adds another €71.50 to it then I immediately have €100 in the account. If I can then find a way to keep this €100 free from the ravages of inflation until I retire, I will receive a significant chunk of it back as tax-free cash and receive an income for life from the

balance, with my spouse receiving a further income if she lives longer than I do. So the question is: how do I best ensure that the €100 does in fact keep pace with inflation? This can be done after careful consultation with your pension adviser by putting in place a strategy that is built around less volatile asset classes, such as an index-linked fund that has at its core holdings such as EU government bonds, or an absolute return fund that seeks to achieve a positive return both when markets are rising and falling. This latter type of fund does, however, require significant research both by your adviser and yourself, as some adopt a much higher risk profile than might appear to be the case on cursory examination.

Thus it is important for all of us to prioritise our pension investments, both in terms of continuing to make them in these tough economic times and also in terms of taking time to ensure that what is known as the 'investment mandate', or overall approach to investment strategy, is one that seeks to ensure that the huge injections of other people's cash into your and my 'living well in retirement fund' is protected, and will still be there for us when the investment market returns to a more stable footing.

### Seizing Opportunities

Of course, once we have minimised risk in our approach to investment, we may then ask questions about how we might seek to seize any opportunities that present themselves in this currently volatile economic climate.

Recently I was lunching with a friend of mine who advises on pension investment strategies with a large firm of private client advisers here in Dublin. I was quite impressed with her approach as she described it:

> Basically, Ian, what I am advising is that clients
> invest their fund into a long-dated German bond,
> yielding a 4.25 per cent return with a redemption date
> of 2025, and then they should re-invest the dividend
> in a basket of shares with a view to capitalising on the
> upturn when it comes, whilst taking no chances with
> their core capital.

See, I was eating at the time, so I was able to chew thoughtfully whilst I worked out what she was saying. And when I did, I really quite liked it.

Essentially, a government bond is like a promissory note to pay you your full capital back on what is known as the redemption date. In the meantime, you will receive income, or yield, on the capital sum. The yield is fixed at the time of purchase and this is what determines the market value of the bond until the redemption date. If interest rates drop below what the bond is offering then its value will rise, and vice versa.

So, in this case, the money would be definitely coming back in 2025; it might have an increased or decreased value, depending on prevailing interest rates at the time. In the meantime, the purchaser would have a small regular income stream with which to seek to take advantage of market volatility and chase potential upside over time. This is one way to play it that's finding a lot of support out there.

There are always opportunities for us to chase, but of course the trick is working out where we might find them. If you do want to take this type of approach, or even to construct your own personal recovery fund of shares that you think might come back well in time, it's worth remembering that:

1. Investing in the market is a long-term project and so you should be prepared to invest and wait, and watch.

2. Jumping successfully in and out of shares is a specialist's game, and a lucky specialist at that, so you should buy with a view to holding your stock for up to five years.

3. You should do a lot of background research and not rely on what some guy said in the pub.

4. You should *never, ever* speculate more than you can comfortably afford to lose, nor should you ever borrow to invest.

There has been a lot of investor interest recently in investing in what are basically earth resources – water, foodstuffs, oil and the like – and on the surface this might appear attractive. Essentially, however, it is important to remember that, whilst in the long term these resources will almost certainly generate strong growth for the investor, in the meantime they are quite volatile and the four principles outlined above will apply equally.

The last area of investing that I want to look at is that of lifestyle investments – investments in artefacts or ideals that not only carry with them the possibility of offering a good return in the long term, but can also enhance our lifestyle in the interim. This category would include such tried and trusted investment areas as wine, first edition books, or, perhaps more commonly, art; but it might also include some more ideologically inspired choices, such as alternative energy companies or other green-issue-based investment areas. There is also a school of thought that says that this current economic downturn creates a good opportunity to invest in small entrepreneur-led niche companies that are seeking to bring new and exciting products to market; products that perhaps reflect the mood of the times in which we live.

It is my view that these are perhaps the type of investments that can bring us most pleasure – and I'm not just thinking about the times when we raid the cellar for a decent red, though those are undoubtedly good times too! You see, for a while in Ireland, perhaps the biggest lifestyle investment opportunity of all, the family home, became almost a commodity to us in the sense that we became so obsessed with value that the provision of shelter, warmth and a base from which to enjoy entertaining our family and friends became almost a secondary objective. But of course now, even though the commodity has fallen in value by over 30 per cent, we can still enjoy all of those other lifestyle benefits.

And it's the same with books, wine and art, and these other lifestyle investments. There's something, for instance, about investing *Dragon's-Den*-like in your brother's latest invention. You know that in all probability it will be money at best returned to you with no increase in value, but just maybe it's the next Reggae Reggae sauce.

The same rules apply though. The ones about not borrowing, and only investing an amount that you know you can comfortably lose, and making sure that you do your research. But if you do the research, and carefully study everything you can find about the investment opportunity, you can have a lot of fun with lifestyle investments.

Even if the answer to my friend's text message question is yes and the WRLD *is* IN REAL BIG TRUBLE.

# A–Z of Recession

**A is for Automobile**

Once upon a time, buying a flashy new set of wheels for the driveway was the recurring desire of Western house-holders, giving birth to the suburban SUV and one even more bizarre status symbol: the convertible that braves the Irish weather in open-top mode. Now nobody wants new cars anymore – and, hey, the money-grabbing developer who built your apartment complex included five parking spaces between two hundred apartments anyway, right?

Where environmentalism failed, the global recession has succeeded: the shine has well and truly faded from the scratched and battered car industry, with the sudden drop in demand creating vast seas of unsold imported cars at ports around the world, as the forecourts overflow with unsold vehicles. By the end of 2008, some of the biggest car makers in the world were approaching governments for state assistance and they were looking for more than just coins for the toll booth: they sought billions in a banking-style bailout. Those who were unsuccessful began putting workers on reduced hours, cutting jobs and letting whirring, screeching production lines fall silent.

## B is for Bonus

Already the subject of much nostalgia and wistfulness, a bonus is a type of payment that is given to workers once a year. Now rare, bonuses were a common phenomenon during boom-era Ireland, with their payment guaranteed to keep the bubbly flowing in bars that embraced a corporate clientele.

Bonuses fell into three overlapping categories, which, in order of ascending size, were as follows: 'Christmas', 'performance-related' and 'executive'. Performance-related bonuses were bonuses used by bosses to reward members of staff they had shared a few pints with during the year. Christmas bonuses were the mass market variety, and were sometimes said to be performance-related, but more often than not they were a one-size-fits-all sop paid to workers by canny employers in a display of seasonal generosity (strictly non-pensionable) that was meant to disguise their stinginess in the other 11 months of the year. Executive bonuses, meanwhile, were always described as performance-related, but like Madonna's marriage to Guy Ritchie, it was a relationship that no one quite understood.

## C is for Credit Crunch

So you don't trust the banks anymore? Well, why should you when they don't even trust themselves? Way back in the heady days of August 2007, the financial crisis known as the credit crunch rocked the global financial system and we've been feeling the lifestyle-crimping reverberations ever since. The credit crunch was characterised by confusion, mistrust and really crap investments related to the US subprime mortgage market. Because financial institutions didn't know and couldn't quite figure out how many bad debts they or their fellow banks had lurking in their broom closets, they became unwilling or unable to lend money to other financial institutions. Without this inter-bank finance, banks that didn't have the cushion of large sums of deposits from savers soon found they couldn't do business anymore. Some banks collapsed, with the first high-profile casualty being British bank Northern Rock (also known as 'Northern Wreck'). Others lumbered on, but found they were exposed to billions worth of debts and had to be bailed out by taxpayers. As the flow of money between the banks dried up, their lending policies became stricter, especially for people and businesses with blemished credit records. Maxed out and miserable, soon we began to experience our own personal credit crunches.

**D is for Deflation**

There is nothing as nice for consumers (although not retailers and their shrinking number of employees) as prices coming down. But deflation has its downside. If the price of goods and services falls rather than rises, the prospect of getting an increase in your pay packet fades, while employers may try to inflict wage cuts. Your day-to-day budget may not be squeezed too much if your cost of living comes down too, but your more modest wages will make the size of your outstanding debts seem stubbornly high. Interest rates may be cut, but only so far – even if you're paying 0 per cent interest on your loans, if your wages fall the size of the debt increases in real terms.

Since this makes you less likely to shell out cash for all that lovely (but unessential) discounted stock in the shop windows, retailers and service providers are forced to drop their prices even further, and thus, over time, the economy sinks into a debt-deflation spiral. The phenomenon is often associated with recessions, including the most famous slump of all – the Great Depression of 1930s America. So yes, after years of complaining about 'rip-off Ireland', soon we may be hoping that the price of stuff starts going *up*.

### E is for Econaclypse

Are you ready for the 'econaclypse'? Coined from 'economic' and 'apocalypse', the word econaclypse was created by technology journalists on the US blog site AllThingsD.com in 2008 to signify the unprecedented financial turmoil and fast deteriorating state of the global economy, as elucidated by hundreds of end-of-the-world-as-we-know-it news headlines documenting/creating the sense of doom and gloom. Examples of econaclyptic headlines include 'Meltdown Monday', 'Market Crash Shakes World', and so on, all of which imply that the stock markets are just one closing bell away from an irreversible financial Armageddon that will send us hurtling back to Great Depression-style soup kitchens, repenting that we ever got carried away by this whole capitalism business.

### F is for Fiscal Stimulus

Overworked, overdrawn, just *so* over it.... You probably feel like a fiscal stimulus right now – it sounds delightfully akin to some higher power handing you a wad of cash with which you can revive your cent-less life, and in a roundabout way it is. A fiscal stimulus is a package of measures used by a government in a bid to resuscitate a flatlining economy. It's like applying cardiac paddles, shouting 'clear' and then standing back to see what happens. It could be a policy intended to prop up consumer spending and protect jobs, such as a cut in taxes (for example, British Prime Minister Gordon Brown's decision to cut the rate of VAT on consumer goods in 2008) or it could be a state investment programme that will create employment (such as US President Barack Obama's infrastructure rebuilding plans).

One problem with these emergency operations is that they leave behind an unpleasant mess. Usually funded by billions of state debt, their eye-watering cost has to be repaid in the years that follow by way of higher taxes. But the main reason why governments, including the Irish Government, don't try to punch their way out of recession by introducing large-scale stimulus measures is because they can't afford them. They're too busy raising taxes just to keep the country ticking over, never mind attempting anything as ambitious as a full recovery.

### G is for Gross National Happiness

A recession is usually defined as two consecutive quarters of negative growth in a country's Gross Domestic Product (GDP), which is a measure of the value of income generated by a country's economy. But with Ireland's GDP and its close cousin Gross National Product (GNP) now contracting instead of growing, does that mean we're less well off? Financially, maybe. But in the Himalayan kingdom of Bhutan, GDP and GNP have been superseded by the concept of Gross National Happiness, a kind of Buddhist version of Western ideas about standards of living. 'Gross National Happiness', first mooted by King Wangchuck in the 1970s, takes into account economic self-reliance, the quality of the environment, the promotion and preservation of national culture, and good democratic governance when deciding how well off people are. It may not be a measure of economic 'progress', but it is one way to assess the population's well-being. As overworked A&E doctors know all too well, earning a good salary isn't the same thing as having a good quality of life.

### H is for *Hello!*

It might seem like just another ream of hairdresser fodder, distinguished from its glossy rivals only by a curious obsession with the polo-playing fringes of the British aristocracy, but *Hello!* magazine can make a material impact on consumer sentiment, according to a 2008 report by the Organisation for Economic Co-operation and Development (OECD). The report found that people who lived in countries where the gap between rich and poor had actually narrowed sometimes perceived the opposite to be true because of the '*Hello!* magazine effect'. The theory goes that when consumers read about the super-wealthy, they feel comparatively worse off as a result.

So next time you pick up a copy of the latest out-pouring of Brangelina-style celebrity smugness, think twice about what such exposure to wealth-powered, continent-hopping lifestyles and nanny-assisted familial bliss may be doing to your already recession-weary mood. On the other hand, to each their own ... pictures of Holly-wood starlets' latest red carpet ensembles might be just the kind of escapist froth you need to put a smile on your face as you grimly sew the button back on your coat.

### I is for Interest Rates

Back in the pre-boom Ireland of the 1980s and early 1990s, interest rates on mortgages in Ireland were as high as 18 per cent, which naturally put a major crimp in the lifestyles of property ladder climbers. The recession that began in 2008 is the first one in Ireland where interest rates are controlled not from Dublin but from Frankfurt, where the governing council of the European Central Bank (ECB) meets once a month to decide whether to increase Eurozone interest rates, cut them or leave them as they are. Slashing interest rates is one way to kick-start a moribund economy, but even when the ECB does decide to lower its key lending rate, it doesn't always follow that borrowers back in Ireland will wind up paying less interest on their loans. That all depends on the type of loan you have, how stingy or generous your lender is feeling and whether or not you're already repaying a mortgage or are thinking of applying for one.

So don't automatically break out the champagne whenever you hear that interest rates have gone down. You may be one of the unlucky ones to whom a rate cut doesn't get 'passed on'. When the ECB increases interest rates, however, you can bet your last euro that Irish banks will find a way of making you suffer.

### J is for Jérôme Kerviel

The French rogue trader became one of the first folk heroes of the financial crisis after he was accused of causing losses of €4.9 billion to his former employer, the bank Société Générale, and triggering a panicky global stock market sell-off in January 2008. For many, Kerviel was not a greedy fraudster, but just the backroom employee who became the fall guy for a widespread culture of irresponsible stock market trading and excessive risk-taking to which senior banking executives had conveniently turned a blind eye. Kerviel's reward was to attract the kind of Internet notoriety that generates legions of Facebook users to set up special groups – such as the one that suggests 'Jérôme Kerviel Should Win the Nobel Prize for Economics' – while T-shirts adorned with the words 'Jérôme Kerviel's girlfriend' duly went on sale.

## K is for Keynes

He died way back in 1946, but the ideas of British economist John Maynard Keynes were influential up until the 1980s and have enjoyed something of a revival thanks to the global financial crisis and economic slump. As shareholders (and the pension fund holders who sit on the sidelines of the stock market) have witnessed to their cost, the vagaries of financial markets don't appear to make much sense – or, as Keynes put it, 'there is nothing so dangerous as the pursuit of a rational investment policy in an irrational world.' Keynes's hostility to a 'casino capitalism' culture was matched by his belief that governments could and should intervene in the economy to counter the negative effects of both boom and bust, rather than just let a free, unregulated market magically work things out for itself. Although Keynesian thinking never completely went away, in the post-crunch era it's come back with a bang.

## L is for Living Standards

Taoiseach Brian Cowen declared in February 2009 that Irish people would have to adjust to a standard of living that is '10–12 per cent lower' than that to which we became accustomed during the boom years. But what does this actually mean? Does this mean we have to buy 10–12 per cent fewer cakes? Will our sofas become 10–12 per cent less comfortable overnight? Standards of living are tricky to measure, but one of the most common ways of assessing them is to keep a watchful eye on Gross

National Product (GNP) per capita. This is the average income of a country's population and gives a quick snapshot of a country's overall wealth. Sadly, Ireland's GNP per capita peaked in 2007 at €36,588, with the Economic and Social Research Institute (ESRI) estimating in December 2008 that this value had already dropped 4.5 per cent in 2008. Ouch.

One weakness in using GNP per capita to measure living standards is that it fails to take into account how wealth is distributed across a population – so while you may find yourself trying to squeeze 10–12 per cent additional days out of your tube of toothpaste, your next-door neighbours may actually be enjoying a boost in their household budget. Most people probably wouldn't care if GNP per capita sank if all it meant was that the super-rich lost a few unnecessary zeroes after their bank balances. But is it going to work that way? No.

**M is for Moral Hazard**

Should governments around the world have 'bailed out' banks using taxpayers' money? In the 'yes' corner, some economists, politicians and commentators argue that, if they had not had done so, the 'systemic risk' to the rest of the economy would have been almost incalculably devastating. If a bank goes (ahem) bankrupt, not only would thousands of its employees all have become unemployed more or less overnight, but the impact would have been felt by depositors, small businesses and other banks. But in the 'no' corner, there are those who point to the 'moral hazard' of the state or central banks stepping in to rescue banks that get themselves into trouble. By supporting financial institutions that have taken massive risks in pursuit of massive rewards, governments are merely legitimising the inappropriate behaviour of the past and encouraging future greed, according to this theory. The banks can now go about their business knowing that the government or central bank will provide a financial safety blanket should the going get tough.

During the credit crunch, fears of moral hazard have tended to be outweighed by fears of complete systemic chaos. This has given rise to the galling but not (yet) revolution-sparking phenomenon whereby profits are privatised (shared by the wealthy few), while losses are nationalised (with everyone having to take the hit). As a taxpayer might say to a senior banker, 'heads you win, tails I lose.'

### N is for Ninja Loan

'Ninja loans' is the industry name for the mortgages shovelled by American banks into the credit-hungry mouths of people with 'No Income, No Job or Assets'. A type of subprime mortgage, they were often drawn down by people with less than perfect credit histories to pay for houses that, as it later turned out, had about as much resale value as a dead geranium. Default rates on these loans escalated from mid-2007, at which point lenders started to serve up eviction notices on their now insolvent prey. The white picket fences of these US subprime suburbs were soon decorated by a mushrooming number of foreclosure sale signs, as the crunch-causing mortgage lenders tried to sell the repossessed properties on to the next sucker.

### O is for Optimism

Fed up with everyone sounding like merchants of doom? Thinking maybe newspaper headline writers have blown this whole economic hiccup out of proportion? Then perhaps a brief snippet of the philosophy of the professionally bumbling Tory soundbite machine, Mayor of London Boris Johnson, is in order: 'Some day, this recession is going to end,' says Boris, a man who is as indefatigable as his tumult of white hair. 'Confidence is going to come surging back with all the biological inevitability of the new infatuation that follows a broken heart.... In the meantime', he continues, 'there's always bicycle hire schemes and bacon sandwiches.'

## P is for Pump and Dump

It sounds like a fun night out, but pumping and dumping is in fact one of the many shady practices employed by stock market vultures who want to make a quick killing. The 'pumping' part is when someone buys a huge number of shares in a company that trades on the stock market and then surreptitiously circulates false rumours that the company is about to do something so amazingly wealth-spinning it will send its share price into orbit. Buyers duly call their dealers to snaffle as many of these 'sure bet' shares as they can afford, which pushes up the share price temporarily. The original rumour-monger then sells or 'dumps' their holding in the stock at the higher price, pocketing the profit. Once this happens, and the company subsequently fails to announce the discovery of Midas-like powers, the price typically falls and investors lose their money.

'Trash and cash' is a similar tactic used by short sellers (who make money when share prices fall), but the whispers they spread are designed to rubbish a company's prospects and make people sell rather than buy a stock. The moral of the story? It's an unscrupulous world out there. Delete any 'hot' or 'urgent' investment tips that land in your inbox and opt for the quiet life instead.

## Q is for Queues

You can tell a lot about the state of an economy by identifying exactly when and where weary members of the general public are waiting in line. Once upon a time, the longest queues in Ireland were made up of pensive, excitable property hunters and snaked around the sides of those now dismantled 'marketing suites' for new apartment complexes, which at the time only actually existed either in the form of architectural drawings or, if you were lucky, miniature scale models with little Lego people looking happy on the manicured lawn. Nevertheless, real estate mania meant that, not only did you have to hand over deposit cheques on properties for which you would have to wait 18 months to get the keys, but you also had to queue to do it. Now that the housing bubble has gone splat and sparked a depressing surge in unemployment, the longest queues can be found outside the dole offices. Such was the influx of people forced to sign on in early 2009 that the waiting times for people to receive their first Jobseeker's Benefit payment stretched from weeks into months in some areas.

## R is for Recessionista

Not to be confused with a 'tight-arse', a recessionista is a woman who instinctively adapts to recession by cutting her costs without ever sacrificing her innate sense of style or joie de vivre. The best things in life may not be free exactly, but a recessionista knows how to have fun on a frugal budget, effortlessly practising the art of 'chiconomics' while the rest of us struggle to make ends meet. She is probably one of those rare people who didn't get carried away by the credit craze in the first place, which is why she finds it so much easier to survive the slump than those flashy money honeys who spent the best part of the

Noughties paying on plastic to take seaweed baths, and now can't adjust to a world where they can no longer afford to keep up costly commitments to professionally assisted depilation. A recessionista is far too busy cycling between supermarkets, farmers' markets and local speciality shops to get the best ingredients for her home-cooked meals to worry about anything as superficial as her personal appearance. This is why it is so damn annoying that her skin radiates such a natural, healthy glow. Want to know how to crunch-proof your life? Ask a recessionista – if you can find one, that is.

**S is for Sterling**

As the sterling-versus-euro exchange rate tipped close to £1 for €1 during the dying days of 2008, crisp pound notes with pictures of the Queen's head on them increased in value for euro-earning shoppers, who promptly crossed the Northern Irish border and bought as much sterling-priced stuff as they could fit in the boot of their cars – then hired a van and went back for more. The weak rate of sterling versus the euro, which has continued into 2009, added to the widely held belief that better prices and deals were to be found beyond the reaches of the 'rip-off Republic', and so shoppers put their fingers in their ears whenever desperate politicians tried to convince them that the 'patriotic' thing to do was to shop at home. But while the weak British currency might have seemed like a lifeline to slump-struck consumers, for Irish retailers and exporters it was a crisis that would cost jobs.

**T is for Toxic**

Toxic has become the catch-all term for worthless assets on the books of financial institutions, which have proved about as corrosive to the global economy as chemical waste is to a nature reserve. Many of these toxic assets originated from clever-clogs lenders in the US who lent sky-high subprime mortgages to people who couldn't afford to repay them, then wrapped up the mortgages into parcels of debt that they gleefully passed on to other financial institutions. For reasons best known to themselves, financial institutions embraced these bad debts onto their balance sheets (or into special 'off-balance sheet' investment funds), not realising that the numbers didn't add up until the whole house of cards came tumbling down.

Irish banks, meanwhile, specialised in advancing large loans to developers to build projects for which they had not yet secured planning permission on land that was rapidly plummeting in value. In the euphemistic world of financial jargon, banks sometimes describe their bad assets as 'impairments' or 'non-performing loans' – a very pretty way of saying that they had dished out a lot of cash and didn't hold too much hope of getting any of it back.

## U is for Unfair

The banks have run amok, the hedge funds have imploded and the Government has blown the boom. So is it fair that humble, diligent workers who never took home spectacular salaries in the first place should now be bearing the brunt of recession? Can it possibly be right that you have to take a 10 per cent pay cut while bank executives still have millions resting in government-guaranteed deposits? How come once upon a time you made an honest, pensionable crust and now you've got even less job security than a Premiership football manager?

Meanwhile, some people claim the credit crunch was actually all of our faults because we overspent and overborrowed. Hmmm. So we bought shoebox apartments at prices that were six times our salaries and used our credit cards so we had a bed to sleep on? We plumped for the iPod Classic in black even though we already had one in white? Does that really compare with bankers who blithely poured millions into black-hole investments and then refused to apologise to taxpayers when they had to rescue them? Of course not: life is unfair. So protest, vote, join a trade union – or just take it lying down if you feel it's not worth complaining – but never let anyone who earns multiples of your salary make you feel guilty.

## V is for Volatility

The laws of gravity mean that what goes up must, eventually, come down. But the stock market is not governed by anything as scientifically reliable as gravity. Instead, share prices lurch wildly in value from one day and one minute to the next, forming delightfully zig-zagging graphs. People whose job title is 'investment analyst' or similar will stare very hard at these graphs until they find, or invent, some kind of pattern. Market volatility increased during the global financial crisis, as banks exhibited less stability than a small child on roller-skates. Seasoned investors who like nothing better than to 'buy low' over breakfast and 'sell high' just as they're contemplating lunch can make tons of money during periods of high 'intraday' volatility. But for most people, a volatile stock market permeated by uncertainty and fear will seem perilously close to being just one whiff of panic away from crashing into the ground. Never underestimate gravity.

## W is for Wall Street

'Greed is good' was the philosophy of Gordon Gekko, the fictional stockbroker portrayed by Michael Douglas in the 1987 film *Wall Street*. It was an ethos readily taken up by a generation of stock market manipulators, hedge fund managers and other financial playboys who migrated to the world's financial industry hubs, including New York's Wall Street, and embraced a lifestyle of unabashed machismo and seemingly consequence-free experiments with trillions of cash, most of which was reassuringly OPM (Other People's Money). Caught up in a bubble of bonuses and Bollinger, the upper echelons of the financial services industry became increasingly divorced from the rest of the world.

This meant that, when the global financial crisis hit in August 2007, many of the most devoted nest-feathering industry insiders remained in a state of shock and denial, refusing to accept that they were not actually *entitled* to earn sums that were 20 times the size of a cardiac surgeon's take-home pay. During the US presidential campaign of 2008, Barack Obama spoke frequently about how the interests and concerns of Wall Street should not be permitted to override those of 'Main Street' – the new term for ordinary folk. As for Gekko, it is often forgotten that he wasn't originally meant to be a role model for capitalism – the concluding act of *Wall Street* shows him getting his comeuppance. Well, Hollywood does love a happy ending.

## xyZ is for Zombies

Banks and companies that are kept artificially alive by massive money transfusions have come to be known as zombies. Although their assets may exceed their liabilities on paper, making them theoretically solvent, zombies are really dead entities running on empty. Everyone knows who they are. Zombie banks are kept on life support machines by the governments who nationalise them, but they can't actually provide businesses or households with the borrowing they need. Zombie companies may be given large cash injections to manufacture goods that nobody wants to buy anymore, usually in order to delay hundreds or even thousands of layoffs. Just like something out of a horror movie, these once-loved zombies stalk the global economy, inadvertently killing non-zombies that fall into their clutches. Take cover.